Wind Grass Hill

and

Other Poems

by Frank L. Gertcher

Black Rose Writing

www.blackrosewriting.com

First printing

ISBN: 978-1-935605-28-7
PUBLISHED BY BLACK ROSE WRITING
www.blackrosewriting.com

Printed in the United States of America

Wind Grass Hill and Other Poems is printed in 12-point Times New Roman

WIND GRASS HILL AND OTHER POEMS

Table of Contents

Table of Contents, Cont...

Table of Contents, Cont...

WIND GRASS HILL AND OTHER POEMS

Table of Contents, Cont...

WIND GRASS HILL AND OTHER POEMS

Table of Contents, Cont...

Dedication

This book is dedicated to Linda, my lovely and caring wife. She inspired many of my poems. Linda also made writing, editing, illustrating and marketing books great fun! Together, we plan to develop other books in the Wind Grass Hill series. What a wonderful way to spend our retirement years!

POEMS AND POETS
(Prologue)

Poets write about their feelings on a topic. An effective poem lets a poet's emotions pass through to the Reader via the medium of language. Yet poems are more; they have design, balance and pattern. Hopefully (from the point of view of the poet) the combination of emotion and structure gives pleasure to the Reader!

This unique book contains 130 poems. Each poem has a short prose introduction that provides context and background. Without being "preachy," some poems address timeless questions of man's relationship to the spiritual world. Is life more than a script already written? Other poems have wry humor and some are just plain fun!

The book is divided into seven chapters. The first chapter presents an epic poem titled: "Wind Grass Hill." The remaining six chapters contain shorter poems. Chapter 2 provides love poems suitable for adults and older children. Chapter 3 playfully presents poems about Disney World; the "young at heart" will love them. Chapter 4 contains poems that reflect on life and spiritual topics, and Chapter 5 contains generally humorous poems about "Travels with Linda." Chapter 6 presents uplifting, sentimental poems under the heading of "Seasons." The final chapter reminisces about growin' up country, and goin' home.

Writing a poem is a personal thing. I designed my poems in old-fashioned "metrical verse" because such forms are comfortable to me. The following brief explanation may give you, the Reader, an understanding of the beauty and balance of this ancient form before you experience my poetry!

Poets of earlier centuries wrote almost exclusively in metrical verse. Most contemporary poets write in 'free form," that is, without the older restrictions of meter and rhyme. I prefer the older form because it is the poetry of my childhood and young adulthood. As a youngster, I avidly read poems by Shakespeare, Milton, Coleridge, Service, Kipling, Longfellow, Tennyson, Riley, Frost and others, including poems by the poet of all young children: Mother Goose! Somehow, to me, the newer free form does not "feel" like poetry.

In metrical verse, each line of a poem can be divided into feet and each foot into stresses, or syllable sounds. The process of dividing a line into metrical feet and each foot into component stresses is called "scansion." An iamb (iambic foot) is one light stress followed by one heavy stress. A trochee is a heavy stress followed by a light stress. A dactyl is a heavy stress followed by two light stresses and an anapest is two light stresses followed by a heavy stress, and so on. A one-foot line is called monometer; a two-foot line is called a dimeter, a three foot line is called a trimeter, a four-foot line is called a tetrameter, etc.

The most common length of a line in English language poetry is pentameter, which is a five-foot line. Thus, "iambic pentameter" refers to a line of poetry that has five feet, with each foot divided into one light stress followed by one heavy stress. This line form was used by Shakespeare in his sonnets, by Milton in "Paradise Lost," etc. The iambic tetrameter form was also used extensively; for example, Robert Frost used it in "Stopping by a Woods on a Snowy Evening," which I memorized as a junior in high school. (Thank you Miss Wallace, you were a great teacher!)

My poems tend to follow either the iambic or trochee tetrameter form and to have lines of the same length (number of feet), but in some cases, the pattern includes lines of slight variation in length to accommodate the "thought" that I try to express. In some poems, I combine lines one and two, three and four, and so on. The result is iambic or trochee "octameter." This rather unusual form condenses the story being told to a smaller space so the reader can scan the whole narrative or easily refer back to a previous point, nuance, etc. without flipping pages. In other poems, I combine two very short lines (three or four words each) into a single line to give the poem a "catchy" rythmn. Thus, and my apologies to the Reader, I occasionally complicate my lines in the interest of more complete expression.

In metrical verse, the most important place in the line is the end and the second most important is the beginning. Let's begin with the beginning!

Most metric poems begin with iambic meter: one light stress followed by a heavy stress. This "soft" beginning sets a relaxed mood. When a poem begins with a heavy stress (trochee, for example), it signals to the Reader that something dramatic will follow! Many of my poems have lines that begin with iambic meter because I want the Reader to feel welcome and "relaxed."

Most often, "rhyme" comes at the end of a line. The similarity of sound at the end of two or more lines creates order to the poem and gives pleasure to the Reader. However, rhyme can also come within a line. I do this in some of my poems because it adds variety and fun! Rhyming patterns include everything from simple couplets (line one rhymes with line two, line three with line four, and so on) to triplets (lines one, two and three rhyme, lines four, five and six rhyme, and so on), to much more complicated rhyming patterns. I occasionally use more complicated patterns, but most of my poems rhyme in couplets. In some cases, I write in iambic meter without end of line rhyme (blank verse), but the rhyme occurs within each line. Oh I have such fun with words!

Some of my poems include variations on a "repeat" line or refrain to provide a rhythmic pattern. The use of a refrain line tends to evoke the pleasure of things occurring and re-occurring. Follow the rhythm!

All poems require a design; part of the enjoyment of reading a poem comes from its sense of orderliness. In a chosen design, all of the concepts discussed above are important: meter, length of line, rhyme and rhythm. Other concepts also matter, including the overall length of the poem, its tone (elegant or casual, extremely casual to include local dialects, etc.), the extent to which imagery is used, and the subject of the poem as a whole.

Part of the design of a poem includes grouping lines into stanzas. Each group of lines, or stanza, is separated by an extra amount of space from the next stanza, or grouping of lines. Stanzas are kind of like paragraphs in prose; a stanza provides a self-contained thought or idea, and then the next thought or idea comes in the next stanza, and so on. The difference in metric poetry (compared to paragraphs in prose) is that each stanza contains the same number of lines as all other stanzas in the poem.

For me, writing a poem is a love affair between the heart and the learned skills of the conscious mind. My feelings on the topic of each poem come from the heart; the metrical verse form that I use to express my feelings comes from learned skills obtained from my teachers and from reading the great poems of the past. I hope you enjoy my efforts, beginning with the first poem titled "Wind Grass Hill."

1. WIND GRASS HILL

Wind Grass Hill is a special place. I go there often, in my mind, before the cold dawn. My hill is a place of spirits, of reflection, of insight. All seekers of wisdom have such a place; whether or not it is called a "hill" is not important.

For me, while on the hill, the myriad details of daily life fade from view. On the distant horizon, the sky does not quite meet the earth, and there are moving shapes in the gray mist. Past, present, and future mix and swirl around me. Alternative paths become visible, and consequences of choice among the many paths become apparent. I see, and I am free to choose. - *Frank Gertcher*

Since the time of Pleistocene ice, generations of Shamans have lived, loved and meditated on and near Wind Grass Hill. The following poem outlines their story. The epic flows from the mind of a present day Shaman as he seeks guidance from the shades of his ancestors. As he meditates, he gradually accepts his present condition and his pre-ordained future. In the poem, you, the Reader, have before you a sweeping vision of a completed circle of life, death, and eternal life. Who is this Shaman!?

Wind Grass Hill

Pale morning comes, chill in the air; walk up the hill, soul burdened with care.
The path is steep, stones hurt my feet; yet I must continue, cold sunrise to greet!
Wind touches hill, sighs soft in the grass, the shades of Shamans, tales from the past.
I seek their memories, ancient yet new, touch on my mind, like fresh morning dew!

Far I have wandered, restless and bold; yet part stayed here, repose for my soul.
Summer now faded, the winter is near; home I've come, seek peace on the hill!
And soon I must go, and find end to my strife, answers I need, the meaning of life.
Time is wasting, cold morning you see; hill spirit please tell me what endings may be!

I will listen; let wisdom words flow; each passing day, my knowledge will grow.
Teach me of earth, red fire, deep waters, how nature works, words of my fathers!
I'll walk on the hill, to boulders that rest, 'tween earth and sky, view from the crest.
The wind in the grass, sighs softly at will; a spirit will speak, through a fox on the hill!

Old fox my friend, amber eyes gleam; tell me your secrets, explain my night's dream.
You are much more than the creature I see; I look in your eyes and visions perceive!
Your eyes to my eyes, your mind to my own, see past, present, future, freedom to roam.
Events occur, along time's golden path; go back then forward, new birth, then death!

Our time moves on, yet lessons foretell; what now is new, that the spirit can tell?
Learn from the past, empty heart fill; now speak spirit, I've returned to the hill!
So far back in time, the memories go; life 'round the hill, the epic does flow.
In swirling mist, both time and space, the stories abound, the spirit keeps pace!

My mind sees a scene: ice, wind and snow, a mega-beast pasture, pale winter glow.
Before people roamed, the trees failed to grow; our hill formed then, an epoch ago!
The spirit walked in wind-driven snow, from heaven sent, to guide and to know.
The spirit had power to do heaven's will; the spirit said: "Let light warm the hill!"

"Let trees grow and great beasts roam, small creatures too, the hill their new home."
Then a voice from above: "O'spirit of hill, man shall come to fulfill heaven's will!"
Man did come, and a few were given, visions and insight and wisdom from heaven.
The few are Shamans; they are here still, hill spirit guides them, shares heaven's will!

The spirit found home back then even so, in the mind of a fox, in bushes so low.
With soft bushy tail and amber for eyes, but Shamans perceived the spirit inside!
A fox on the hill, with heaven's insight, Shamans greet foxes, share wisdom's light.
All Shamans see visions; through a fox behold, dreams become real, stories unfold!

Shamans found wisdom, this they shared; hunters and gatherers, people who dared;
The hill, the forest and rivers so cold, they dressed in warm skins, adventurers bold!
Wild scene evolved; green covered ground, fur-clad people, the night closed 'round.
They heard Shaman's tale, by fire low flicker, children of old, hearts beat quicker!

The cold climate warmed; hill weathered slow; trees grew by hill, creatures below,
Rain and warm breezes, soft green the glow, gentler times, more sun than snow!
High Eagle Shaman with Storm his wife, they struggled to fill a village with life,
Corn was their crop, up from the south: new ways prospered, not hand to mouth!

Shamans adapted, knowledge passed on, father to daughter, then daughter to son,
Hunters turned farmers, villagers did see; crops filled the larders, the future will be!
New people came, from the far south, Shamans taught wisdom; words changed doubt.
New people built cities, wondrous things; trade fostered deeds, business of kings!

Villagers to the city, Cahokia did grow; kings fought for land, made wars ebb and flow.
A Shaman was old, sought help from youth; granddaughter listened, lessons in truth!
Nightbird her name, eyes steady gaze, she walked with Shaman, warm summer days.
Shaman told of the sun, the moon and reasons, why shadows fall, changes of seasons!

Shaman had reasons for Nightbird to grow, too old to travel, his message to sow.
The war blighted the land; the innocent cried; the old king was dead; rivals did vie!
The new king was young; he needed advice; to shape a new order, killing must cease.
Old Shaman knew how, but flesh was weak; he needed help; his message to speak!

Nightbird listened; Shaman's words did flow; each passing day, knowledge did grow.
He taught about earth, red fire, deep waters, how nature worked, words of his fathers!
She walked on the hill, to boulders that rest, 'tween earth and sky, view from the crest.
The wind in the grass, sighed softly at will; a spirit did speak, through a fox on the hill!

Nightbird perceived; fox eyes gleamed! "Tell me secrets; explain Shaman's dreams!
You are much more than the creature I see; I look in your eyes and visions perceive!
Your eyes to my eyes, your mind to my own, see past, present, future, freedom to roam.
Events occur, along time's golden path; go back then forward, new birth, then death!"

Nightbird learned what all Shamans knew; from spirit on hill, time passed in review.
She walked paths, learned about places, then back to Shaman and his good graces!
In her eighteenth summer, she met a young man; love at first sight, he held her hand.
Her mate matched her well, Free Hawk his name, steady and brave, a hunter of fame!

Young love and passion, souls of like mind, warm on the grass, bodies entwined.
The old Shaman did know; their secret he kept; under the stars, young lovers slept!
Nightbird had wisdom, soft on her voice; Free Hawk had courage, they made a choice.
With stars in their eyes, sure of truth, Shaman's eyes twinkled, remembered lost youth!

Nightbird and Free Hawk listened to tales, adventurous youth, a yearning to ease,
Visions of cities, high houses, great kings, bright torches alight, eagles on wings!
Shaman told Nightbird, in daytime swoon, that sun would darken, covered at noon.
He knew the day and how it would be; when the sun hid its face, people would flee!

Foretold in dreams, Shaman's old head, report from ancestors, Shamans long dead.
Then Nightbird obtained the memories you see, eclipse of the sun, how it would be!
The strife must stop; the king must agree; old Shaman knew; Nightbird did see;
How to convey this, a way was found; Nightbird and Free Hawk, Cahokia bound!

Road they found, heading straight west; Cahokia waited, they needed no rest.
Avoid cruel warriors; come to the city, King's festival time, crowds in a frenzy!
Young king looked down; his spirit was low; enemies lurked in crowds down below.
He wanted peace and his rivals to end, their fight for control of people and land!

A sign from above, so rivals would bow, to king and religion, find a unity power.
Peace once started, his rivals would hear, his plan to share power among noble peers!
Nightbird and Free Hawk arrived in the square; skirted the crowd, an unlikely pair.
At the base of the mound, Free Hawk did cry: "A sign from above, look to the sky!"

Nightbird climbed on the mound's near side: "Sun will diminish, you cannot hide!"
Warriors started toward this strange pair, but shadows grew, along with their fear!
The young king stood, his voice did shout: "I see an omen, listen and doubt.
Now come up to me, maiden so fair; tell me the truth, the darkness I fear!"

Nightbird cried: "Shaman message you need, sun will diminish and return if you heed;
Bring peace to the land, rivals must end, their fight for control of people and land!"
The crowd stood quiet, darkness at noon; Nightbird climbed up, in deepening gloom.
She quietly explained Shaman's fair dream; the King understood; message received!

King turned to crowd, voice strong and clear: "Maiden told me when sun re-appears.
It will stay only if you all share the land, share peace and goodwill, rivals must end!"
The crowd cried: "Yea! Let sun return!" Warriors did pause, now purpose uncertain.
King seized the moment, Nightbird in tow, ordered a council for sharing the power!

Far away on the hill, Shaman did smile; his message delivered; all was worthwhile.
Nightbird and Free Hawk would prosper and build; he could rest; his life fulfilled!
Nightbird and Free Hawk, their future assured, peace in the land, adventures reward.
The new Shaman was she, advisor to king; counselor was he, strong spirit and deeds!

Slow centuries passed, wind blew a change, and new men arrived, trappers of game.
The old ways faded, the Shamans did see; must adapt or perish; the future will be!
See dusk on the hill; feel chill on the breeze, fall of the year, red and gold leaves.
Generations passed since Cahokia time; new people new ways, what does it mean?

A woman by firelight, Shaman was she, pondered the future, great changes did see.
Her companion a trapper, eyes steady gaze, he loved this woman; he learned old ways!
She told him of earth, red fire, deep waters, how nature worked, words of her fathers.
He told her of people across a broad sea, of ships and trade and days that would be!

Others would come, cabin and farm; the hill would see change; would there be harm?
Yet somehow they knew; this too would pass; the hill would remain, as in the past!
More people came, built cabins and farms; the hill saw change, good and the harm.
The Shamans adapted; frontier had changed; tried to end wars, councils arranged!

Shaman's son Nathan, grown and wise, defended his cabin, wife and daughters inside.
He quickly stepped out, strong hands held a rifle; steady his purpose, fire in his eyes!
Spied out a target, long rifle to shoulder, aimed small and fired, enemy dropped over.
Then quick draw a pistol, he fired to the side, an enemy fell; two now had died!

Battle in earnest, bullet struck home, Shaman's son stumbled, death has arrived.
Defender now down, screams from inside, wife followed husband, courage her guide!
More shots cracked; brave wife sighed, darkness enveloped; she then could not rise.
She fell by husband, blood on the ground, warriors triumphed, though price very high!

See the old Shaman, heart stabbed in pain, his mind found grief, saw death in dream!
Nightmare at dawn, son's spirit cried out: "Father come quickly, daughters remain!"
Old but strong, Shaman made journey; back to the hill, found neighbors on way.
East on the trail, the sunrise glowed red, smoke in distance, a pyre for the dead!

Bold rescuers grim, Shaman did lead; with rifles in hand, great was their speed!
A somber arrival, took care of the dead; then followed the trail, captives to save.
Warriors to village with captives in lead, shouted to village, proud of their deed.
Triumph was small, few captives to show; two little girls, their parents laid low!

An old man emerged, Chief of the village, kin to the Shaman, saddened by pillage.
Admonished warriors, evil their deeds: "Revenge breeds revenge, why don't you see?!"
The Chief and the Shaman, long, long ago, listened to stories by campfire's red glow.
Grandfather taught them, wisdom their goal, youngsters together, friendship did grow!

Observed the captives; kin from afar, honor and duty; save Shaman's Granddaughters.
"Take them inside; they're not to be sold!" Warriors were angry, but feared to answer!
Action needed; Chief removed halters; he quickly adopted Shaman's Granddaughters.
Cowed by the Chief, warriors gave way; children were grateful, wait for Grandfather!

Two days passed for Chief and children, warriors had left, more smoke on horizon.
Followed their trail, rescuers saw village, Shaman's hope, avoid battle and pillage!
Shaman sat silent, to wonder of friends, nearby the village he waited for signs.
A dream came, his plan now made, Shaman said: "Wait! Alone I will win!"

Friendship respected, Shaman was wise, forces deployed, to guard from surprise.
The warriors away, but they might return; Shaman moved in, alone at sunrise!
Granddaughters waited, somehow they knew; Grandfather's coming; confidence grew.
The Chief and his wife planned this alliance; old friend arrived, near village in silence!

Chief and Shaman, met at woods edge: "Children are ready, go quickly my friend!"
Few words spoken, yet meaning learned: "Take children now, before warriors return!"
Shaman's message to boyhood friend: "Join us in flight, warriors won't understand!"
Chief smiled, his eyes twinkled and gleamed: "I will stay here, my duty, your need!"

"I will buy time, you may gain distance, I know the danger, but I take the chance;
Soon we will meet, friendship enhance, on Wind Grass Hill, our spirits will dance!"
"The near future I see, old friend so fair; your duty is clear; more grief I now bear!"
Nodded agreement, Granddaughters in tow, Chief to village, Shaman journey to go.

Tireless on trail, Shaman their guide, friends and Granddaughters, warriors avoid.
Deep pain in memories, grief later to share, son and old friend, both lost to a war!
Battles continued, whites slowly did win, Shaman mediated, saved lives in the end.
Though heavy his heart, his duties did wait, Granddaughters need, orphaned by fate!

He rebuilt cabin, home for Granddaughters, time healed hearts, child's love answered.
He gave Shaman memories; many stories did tell; years in review, family fared well!
Shaman told girls of earth, fire and waters, how nature worked, words of his fathers.
Time passed on, smiles dawned new, girls learned to farm, and to womanhood grew!

The girls listened; Shaman's words did flow; each passing day, knowledge did grow!
They walked the hill, to boulders that rest, 'tween earth and sky, view from the crest!
The wind in the grass, sighed softly at will; a spirit did speak, through fox on the hill!
Events occurred along time's golden path, back and then forward, birth, then death!

The fox was their friend, his eyes gleamed; he shared secrets, explained their dreams!
He was much more than the creature they saw; looked in his eyes and visions foresaw!
His eyes to their eyes, his mind to theirs, see past, present, future; memories to share!
Both girls learned what all Shamans knew, from spirit on hill, time passed in review!

One evening quiet, old Shaman dreamed; son and old friend, on horizon did seem.
"Hello kindred spirits! Join you I will! Now is the time for our dance on the hill!"
Old Shaman passed, but shade remained, a wind on the hill, a voice in a dream!
One girl grew old, Esther by name; she learned from the tales, Shaman became!

Now forward in time; the country grows; I must tramp the hill; the epic flows!
Shamans continued; born and grow old, Esther's shade my guide; her stories unfold!
Esther told me: "Upon the hill, there is a place, the spirit sighed and touched my face;
My mind soared free and it drifted along; a soft warm breeze brought nature's song!"

"And peace I found; cruel memories passed, and they sighed away amid the tall grass;
Away high on the hill it seemed so real, the spirit spoke softly, and my soul did heal!
Open your heart and peace you will find, the spirit will speak so soft to your mind!"
I listened to Esther; so real it seemed, and walked to the place foretold in my dream!

Then Esther told me of love ever after, of John her husband, and Lizzy her daughter.
How the world was new when Lizzy was small, the cabin was warm, the trees so tall!
How she would sing to Lizzy, in a voice so sweet, Lizzy gave smiles, her special treat.
Through her childhood years, warm summer nights, Shaman words gave her delight!

"Lizzy learned of sun, the moon and reasons, why shadows fall and flowing seasons.
Then came the time for Lizzy to meet, a strong stalwart boy, my Princess sweet!
I had to let go, my child had grown; her mind did hold the seeds that I had sown.
Young love did weave its magic spell; her time was short, but she used it well!"

"Three babies born, Sam, Sarah and Lynette, a loving home, Lizzy gave her best.
But Lizzy died young, and I was left lonely, with her husband, to raise her family!
Then I walked from woods, solemn and dim, to my refuge hill, sunny and green.
Like you I wanted heart pain to cease, sought spirit on hill, found rest and peace!"

"Then the children grew, and Sam was special; he walked the hill and met the foxes;
And Sam listened; let wisdom words flow, each passing day, his knowledge did grow.
I taught him of earth, red fire, deep waters, how nature works, words of Grandfather!
He walked on the hill, to boulders that rest, 'tween earth and sky, view from the crest."

"The wind in the grass, sighed softly at will, a spirit did speak, through fox on the hill.
The fox was his friend, amber eyes gleamed; he told secrets, explained night dreams!
Sam's eyes to fox eyes, his mind was sown, with visions of future, freedom to roam.
And young Sam found a place, a deep cave in stone, only we knew; our secret alone!"

"Then Sam grew up; I passed away, and Sam marched to a war, cold winter's day.
Found victory in battle but mourned loss of life; returned from war, found loving wife!
Sam walked on the hill; he built a new life; then a fight on the bridge, a time of strife.
Bad men were killed, Sam took their gold; he hid it away, in the cave he had found!"

Now Esther's voice faded, the story you see, was already known, my father told it to me.
Sam was great grandfather; he lived long ago, Civil War times, he hid Shaman gold!
Sam knew the future, gold he saved; it was meant for hard times, deep in his cave!
Hard times brought need, my father you see, found Sam's gold, so future could be!

When father was young, fancy roamed free, he lived on the Wabash; as he told it to me.
Later the Depression brought want and harm; father was needed back on the farm!
But that was later when he settled down; with wife and children, returned to the farm;
And money was needed, farm to re-build; Shaman tales told him where to find gold!

Earlier on the Wabash, prohibition in force, wild hard living, moonshine of course!
He was only sixteen in the year '26, and way down on the river, he lived by his wits!
He arrived by steam train, boxcar by choice, far from the farm, to give his heart voice.
Now listen my friend, see story unfold, like I heard many times, adventures so bold!

He described a train: "a chariot of fire, belching black smoke, so high in the air!
New sights and sounds, just over the hill, far out on the rails, to go where I will!
View from a boxcar, from farm I go, pastures and cornfields speed by my door!
The river calls me; it's off to the west, find swift brown water, my mettle to test!

Train slowed for bridge, pack out the door; jumped from the train, wheels make a roar!
I went to a spring; washed soot from my hair, sounds of the river, sweet on the air!
Upstream to cabin, a friend I must meet, home on stilts, nets hung from trees.
Smoke from chimney, wispy and white, Hannibal's there, drunk from last night!

It's sour mash a'cookin', still to the right, moonshine a'makin', aged overnight.
Samplin's a duty, Hannibal takes care, make sure it's right, before he will share!
No cares or ties, simple and light, sell fish and brew, enough for each night.
Fishing and brewing, oh what a life, with Hannibal Jones, river rat knight!"

Three years with Hannibal, oh what fun, but then the crash, Depression begun.
The stock markets down, hard times new born, the banks fail; savings all gone!
No job, no money, just sign on relief; hear the cry in street: "How can we eat?"
The fields dry, dust blows, no rain today, crops die, child cries, hope fades away.

Rich all hide, they hoard scarce cash, the poor starve, all desperate and rash.
Then the troops march, no bonus to pay, bitter words, and homes burn away.
Where's God? Please help! No answer; desperate the cry: "How can we eat?"
It was time to go home, return to the fold; Shaman tales told where to find gold!

A tumble down house at end of a lane, see faded colors and cracked window pane.
Brambles and leaves fill an overgrown lawn, broken gate path, all muddy and brown.
Trees needed pruning; dormant and bare, weeds lined a fence, needed trim and care.
Outbuildings showed sag, the paint peeled away, windows opaque, dust lined the glaze.

Power line drooped from transformer pole; birds perched on line, all silent in row.
No songs, no cheer, just wind's mournful sigh, silent and cold, a farm ready to die.
Pale light shined through kitchen side door, old man stepped out, to tend daily chores.
Wife waited inside, farm breakfast prepared; life dimly flickered, worn, deep cares.

Past summer ghosts stand here and there, lament the sad state and need for care.
Youth must return, to build and repair, search out meaning, seek answers to prayers.
My father stood, his back to the dawn, observed the farm, sad, hopeless, forlorn.
His purpose was clear, life must renew; farm must survive, and prosper anew.

Across the road, fox watched from hill, Shaman returned, strong hands, strong will.
The fox blinked his eyes, the night had passed; he silently faded in tall winter grass!
Find the gold! Like many before, my father stood alone on the hill, quiet his mood.
In his dream on the hill, he saw a cave; a boy stood inside, in candle light wave!

The cave scene faded; he then saw five men; they stood on a bridge, faces were grim!
Then four shots rang out; three fell on the span; two remained, and one was Sam!
The dead men were thieves, from farmers extorted; Sam and his kin a robbery aborted!
Sam found fortune in gold; no way to return; Sam hid the gold, for the future to earn!

In my father's dream, cave was found, he knew where to look; a small entrance round.
Gold was there, and a friend from old days, knew how to fence it, with cash walk away!
The farm restored, it prospered indeed, from desperate to affluent, no longer in need.
Through good times and sad, farm by the hill, a future for Shamans, path will fulfill!

Now I am the Shaman; father has passed; I look to the future, but remember the past;
And I walk on the hill to sooth troubled soul, and the future I seek, a golden path flow!
The fox is here, spirit's eyes gleam; hear my sigh! Show me a path; words to live by!
Words from the spirit! Clear as a bell! I pass them to you; remember them well!

"Your parents knew that death must come; yet they lived each day, faced rising sun;
Now they are gone; heaven's delight, yet they dream with you, deep in the night!
Our Lord in heaven, knows grief you bear, seek out his hand, he waits; he cares!
Future will bring new faces, new dreams, life will continue, hard it now seems.

You must adapt, find end to strife, you must continue, seek love in your life!
Now open your heart; I'll show you a way; seek happy times; love every day!
World goes on, you've walked on the hill; found life's wisdom, accept Lord's will!
Embrace each sunrise, seek wisdom at night, the future comes, follow the light!"

I'll now leave the hill; to ponder a bit, the spirit was special, bold wisdom his gift.
I'll never forget; morning's dim light, old Shaman memories and heaven's insight!
Winter comes, yet while light gleams, I'll find the meaning in Shamans' old dreams.
The far future I see, my soul wanders still, I'll join kindred shades with spirit on hill!

Wind will touch hill, sigh soft in the grass, my soul at peace, with tales from the past.
Others will seek; words ancient yet new, I'll touch their minds, like fresh morning dew!
Then my shade will wander, restless and bold, in rippling grass, untouched by the cold.
New Shamans walk; old questions appear, seeking my counsel; find peace on the hill!

And the spirit remains, as a fox on the hill; he's forever a guide; to all seekers fulfill;
And I see a line of new Shamans who wait, in the gold light, at heaven's high gate!

Again, who is this Shaman? Readers, look deep into your souls, do you see gleaming eyes, a Shaman within? May you find peace on your hill, make wise choices, and obtain joy in your life! Open your heart; you will find a way; seek happy times; love every day!

2. LOVE POEMS

Love is fragile and complex; it is hard to explain; it is expectation, passion, and refuge from pain. It is kindness and warmth, a desire to respond, planning and sharing, a will to move on!

Romantic love becomes "real" through personal experiences. Although such experiences are unique in detail, they usually have general themes that resonate with the romantic experiences of others. Because of the similarities, poets can express love stories with universal themes that touch the heartstrings of many readers. In turn, readers fill in their own unique details. As a result, love poems can cause smiles or tears and raise hopes and fears in receptive hearts. Perhaps the following poems will bring smiles, hope, and fond remembrance!

Expectation

I'll walk in my garden, in dew-fresh garden,
Where honeybees dance and make sweet romance
With flowers that perfume the breeze.

I'll wait for my lover in sun-lit garden,
Our souls will unite and dreams will take flight
To succor, to guide, and to please.

I want to begin, in sweet quiet garden,
Life's endless quest to meet every test
Together, with trust and belief.

See secluded bench, within my garden?
Where hearts find rest and lovers caress
And answers fill every need!

Love can be funny, if you are an objective observer. Youngsters, especially teenagers, sometimes take attractions to the opposite sex too seriously! Boys so want to impress girls, and vice versa. Sometimes, in their own eyes, everything they try turns out wrong!

Girls!

Girls with curls and flashes and swirls,
Bright eyes, whispers and feminine guiles.
Soft curves, graces, and smiling young faces,
Slow walk, small talk, uncomfortable places!

World now complex, a whole new game,
Drawn to their presence, a moth to the flame!
What should I do as they giggle and coo,
Bow down, don't touch, or hide in the loo?

I want to say things that excite and impress,
How to do that is anyone's guess!
Tongue mixes round, it comes out wrong,
An awkward mumble instead of a song.

Girls stare and laugh, ruin my whole day,
Look over shoulders, as they walk away.
I stand in the hall, blushing pale red,
Look for a hole, the future I dread!

What should I do in the presence of girls?
Girls with curls and flashes and swirls?
I think I'll go home and hide in my bed,
My head under pillow, wish I was dead!"

Believe it or not young man, the time will come when you will find that special girl. So it was with me, so long ago! When I was young, church on Sunday provided opportunities to meet girls and yes, fall in love! Church sounds old-fashioned, but such settings still provide opportunities. Church is a good place!

Silver Path

A lovely girl, but does she know, a future lies in silver glow?
She looks at me, a puzzled smile; can I win her love somehow?

We meet in church, a wholesome place, she dresses nice, a lovely face!
How do I show that I do care? Shall I speak? What can we share?

After church, she counts the funds, offerings made, collection's done.
I offer help, she smiles and says, "OK by me, count coins today!

Roll them up, I'll count the bills, we'll add the take, a bag we'll fill.
Keep in safe, for bank in morn, thank you kindly, you're quick to learn."

Now each week, we meet, I say, "Can I help count coins today?"
"OK by me," she smiles and says: "we'll work together, quick that way."

A month goes past, she smiles and waits; how do I ask for our first date?
I finally get the nerve to ask, "Will you go with me this Saturday night?"

"A movie plays that you might like, I'll borrow car, for your delight.
It's not much, but I hope you'll see, I want you so, on date with me!"

She says "OK, I might go, what's the name of the picture show?"
I stutter, blush, forgot the name, she smiles and says: "I'm ready at eight."

I pick her up, at ten 'til eight, she's ready to go, it's heaven's gate!
We talk and talk at the picture show, she laughs at jokes, her eyes aglow.

I drive her home, but I get lost, one-way streets, confuse us both.
We make it home, hour is late. She smiles and says "I enjoyed our date!"

My heart rides high, she must know; a future lies in silver glow!
I love her face, her knowing smile; I hope to win her love somehow!

Lovers meet in church or otherwise, fall in love, and experience all of the ups and downs of romance! If everything falls into place, the happy couple gets hitched!

Every lover looks forward to that special night, after the wedding, and you are alone with the one you love. Such special moments live forever in our memories!

Passion

An open door in swirling void, pale gold light, sweet calm voice.
Hesitant steps, I look within; a figure moves, tall and slim.

A silhouette and background glow, sensual moves, smooth and slow.
Light moves round, details of grace, a woman's form, a smiling face.

If I reach out, will she remain? I fear to touch, the dream may fade.
Warm hand finds my trembling own, no need to fear, love will grow!

She moves to me, our bodies touch, glowing skin, warm with love.
Tender moves, like love's first kiss, a sweet caress, a drift to bliss!

I move my hands along her sides, I see her smile, and close her eyes.
Her hand moves down and I respond, passion slow, the timeless round!

We tender move from kiss to kiss, caress so sweet, the height of bliss.
We fade to rest, warm afterglow, no need to fear, our love does grow!

Honeymoons have many special moments. In addition to laughter, warm caresses, the best wishes of friends, and finally, time alone, there are moments for reflection. Do you remember a quiet time; early in the morning, after a very special night? I do!

Good Morning!

Our room is cool, our bed is warm,
I feel you breathe and caress your arm.
My eyes open, yours stay closed,
We both smile and we both know.

I'm wide awake in dawn's pale light,
Outlined by window, an end to night.
I think of day, what we might do,
A precious moment, soft next to you!

You stir and stretch, I know you wake,
I brush your hair and touch your face.
Eyes slow open, they sparkle bright,
Eyes that know our love's delight!

You start my day, fulfill my dream,
We rise from rest, survey the scene.
A bright new sun, the night has passed,
Shadows gone, our day at last!

When evening comes for two lovers, anticipation can be a wonderful thing. They go to bed, and they drift to a land of special dreams! Do you remember?

Dreamers

The night flows 'round, warm bed awaits,
Perchance we'll dream, trust to our fates!
Our heavy eyes close; now lie next to me,
Slow drift to sleep, dreamers we'll be!

A path now forms, from swirling mist,
Along it we glide, seek lover's bliss.
Gate in the distance, see yonder light?
Soft golden haze, our senses delight!

Downy as feathers, float up in the air,
Spin slowly 'round, fade away care!
Look down to earth, spread all below,
Cool white mist in moonlight glow!

Lovely to see, your green and white gown,
Breeze in your hair, silver your crown!
Gown turns wispy, your silhouette shows,
Sensual form, from head to your toes!

Your eyes open, soft ruby lips,
I touch your cheek, gently we kiss.
Soar higher and higher, hear angels sing,
Hearts find freedom, souls take wing!

Touching and laughing, float on the breeze,
Bodies entwine; our passions to please!
Senses all tingle, up, up we soar,
Starburst a-twinkle then sparkles float low!

Slowly we drift, down through the air,
Relaxing and glowing, sensations we share!
Down through the night, stars up above,
Dreamers we were, special our love!

Toes touch the earth, golden path waits,
Back we must glide, to distant gate.
Stillness of night, lovers' dream fades,
Return to the bed, warmly we lay!

Night flows 'round, velvet and smooth,
Souls at rest, sleep we now choose.
Remember our love, warm next to me,
Soon we'll return, dreamers to be!

Wine and roses, walks in the moonlight, playful lovemaking, ah, the honeymoon, such sweet remembrance! Unfortunately, honeymoons end. Then it is back to work and to responsibilities. Oh, what we would give for just a few more days!

Honeymoon's Over!

Return from the wedding, stars in our eyes,
Review all the pictures, warm smiles, sweet sighs!
Back to routines, no longer the rover,
Bills flow in, the honeymoon's over!

Remember room service? All in the past,
Now we fix breakfast, wolf it down fast!
Back to our jobs, our diets do suffer,
Donuts and coffee, honeymoon's over!

Bathroom's a mess, toothpaste on mirror,
Shower needs cleaning, the toilet whatever!
No maid stops by, no sparkle to savor,
Must clean it ourselves, honeymoon's over!

Lawn wants mowing, edges need trim,
Work in the garden, weeds clearly win!
No gardener comes 'round, fingers get blisters,
Backaches on weekends, honeymoon's over!

Wish we could go, backward in time,
Re-live the moments of roses and wine!
Though we miss days, walk in high clover,
We still have each other, tho' honeymoon's over!

Newly married couples must adjust to each other's habits and preferences. Methods of adjustment are often amusing, especially with regard to use of leisure time. Men and women are "wired" differently!

Movie and reading preferences provide two good examples. Women tend to like "chick flicks" and "chick lit." Men prefer action movies and non-fiction "how to" books. Women tend to ignore men folk when they watch an old John Wayne movie; they usually go into another room and talk on the phone, or more likely, go shopping! Men mostly fall asleep when forced by circumstance to watch a chick flick. It is certainly true that they have other things in mind when the wife reads a chick lit novel in bed!

Chick flick movies usually match the heroine against a man who has emotional problems of some sort. However, they work together to put the "villain" away. A rocky romance ensues. In the end, they get married. Male reaction to the movie: Why not skip to the ending and be done with it?

Chick Flick Tonight!

We rent a video for evening fun,
Wife picks the movie, that's how it's done!
Bold action and westerns not her style,
She wants a chick flick, with feminine guile!

So chick flick tonight, whether or no,
Now sit on the couch; start up the show!
The wife all a-twitter, I'm just resigned,
Grin and bear it, though sleep is in mind!

Movie now starts, super chick smiles,
The men all stare, line up in files!
Flounces and bounces, men on the spot,
A silly sound track, no trace of a plot!

High fashion reigns, lovers find cupid,
Super chick wins, men mostly stupid!
The movie drones on, eyelids droop,
Sleep my escape, too bored to move!

Wife on the couch; she looks my way,
She shakes her head; then has her say!
"The movie is great, don't you enjoy?"
"Of course, my dear, girl gets the boy!"

"Just resting my eyes, movie is great!"
Wife raises her eyebrows, ponders my fate,
Rent chick flicks forever, an endless run,
The wife always wins, that's how it's done!

Chick lit novels are like chick flick movies, except that they take longer to finish. Women read the novel, cry and sniffle a lot, and then recommend the novel in glowing terms to their female friends. Occasionally, they try to describe the plot to a man. This is always a lost cause, for three reasons: first, the plot is incomprehensible to begin with and cannot be described in a rational conversation; second, the novel is about female emotions, which are also incomprehensible, and finally, a man cannot possibly be expected to understand a novel that doesn't have a John Wayne type as the main character!

Chick Lit

A female thing, a novel that swings from silly to depressingly drastic,
Heroine obsessed and tries her best, in a plot that's completely fantastic!
Her world is all gray, great passions at play, the villain she must defeat,
Sex steamy and money, high fashion a-plenty, murders litter the street!
Time fritters away, but wifey just lays, reading all evening in bed,
Hear the sighs, tears in her eyes, her brain cells dying or dead!

Book jacket describes what's inside: Engaging! Accessible! Must read!
Sublime the plot! Compelling subplots! Readers all anxiously heed!
The novel's text has a lead-in to next, words that urge reader to look,
For author's name, publisher's game, trying to sell their next book!
Males prefer play, but females stay, hooked on book series you see,
They love to sigh, a tear in the eye, continuous fantasy to please!

Her books form a pile, soon out of style, one read is more than enough,
She'll pass books on, hither and yon, other females just love this stuff!
Occasionally look over top of her book, maybe she's fallen asleep,
But probably not, engaged in the plot, found fantasy world so deep!
Just watch TV news, paying my dues, events important to dread,
Might as well sigh, while wifey just lies, reading her novel in bed!

Time passes; lovers adjust to married life, and they begin to look inward; two people become one. Lovers plant flowers that grow and blossom. They face the world with single purpose. Sometimes a wall must be built to protect the flowers. Such walls take time to build, and seasons pass.

Garden Wall

We'll finish a wall to circle our flowers,
Protect the same from rambling wild.
We started last year; we poured the concrete,
A smooth stone face will make it complete.

Winter has come with snow all around,
It blankets our garden, white frozen ground.
Survey the scene and wait for next spring,
To finish our wall and new flowers bring.

I close my eyes and clearly see,
Dream flowers wait for you and me.
Silent time now, grey wall on white,
Yet spring will come and new flowers delight!

We'll finish the wall, with golden stone face,
We'll plant flowers, in the protected space.
Colors will fill the now naked beds,
New life will grow from nothingness.

When wall is done, we'll trim and clip,
Our glorious flowers and relationships!
Strong stone will circle, rich golden brown,
Protect our flowers that cover the ground.

Seasons come, seasons pass. Flowers and dreams come to fruition and then fade. Yet there are always a few blossoms in the fall, and the intermittent sunshine takes on a golden hue!

September Garden

Our garden fades, few blossoms remain,
Soft breeze cool, a forecast for rain.
Gray clouds pass, swiftly they flow,
Fall has arrived, with promise of snow.

Special our garden, just you and me,
A dream time garden, to love and to be!
Quiet we've earned, mid rustle of leaves,
Peace in our garden, hold hands with me!

Our hearts at rest, no fetters, no past,
Just this moment, forever to last!
Golden our path, new dreams to fulfill,
Savor our moment, before winter's chill!

Cares fade away, no movement, no sound,
Gold path awaits, soft light all 'round!
Look in my eyes, what do you see?
My soul peers out, longing for thee!

Have you ever been alone in your room at night, and your lover is far away? In every generation, there are wars that separate lovers; hearts are lonely, and fear of the unknown weighs heavy on those who wait at home.

Sounds in the Night

Evening comes, with sounds of the night,
Katydids trill, in the silver moonlight.
Whippoorwills call, soft sigh the breeze,
Reminds me of you, now far overseas!

Moments we spent on the old porch swing,
Listening to sounds that evening brings.
We talked of our day, made plans for the morn,
Such simple things, I miss more and more!

Bedtime comes, and new sounds add,
Call of an owl, and rustlings in grass.
Crickets sing low for mates in the dark,
Like them I miss my distant sweetheart!

Past times we walked from porch to our room,
We listened to sounds and looked at the moon.
I held your hand; you gave me a smile,
Such simple things, I miss more and more!

Past love a memory, but future love waits,
Now each alone, our yearning hearts fate.
I send my love, on soft evening breeze,
To you it will flow, across the broad sea!

During times of prolonged separation, thoughts and prayers transcend time and space. Communications between lovers occur, even across vast distances. Modern day cell phones and computers with E-mail are not needed; just remain quiet, close your eyes, and let your mind roam free!

I Miss You!

A faraway place I see in my dream,
You sleep alone, and I do the same.
I long for your smile, the warmth of your touch.
I know we must wait, I miss you so much!

Soft breeze sighs near window this night,
Do you hear its sound, as we wait for the light?
Night breeze turns round, my voice on its wing,
To you it will wend, my love it will sing!

Listen and know the breeze softly tells,
Of home and warmth, and my love as well.
Walk in our dream that we share each night,
This war will end, and we'll meet in the light!

My thoughts reach out, I know you see,
My smile and hand as you dream of me.
Hold on the dream and smile as you wake,
Your heart I do keep, be sure of its fate.

As you rise from your dream, tasks you must do,
Please think of return, our lives to renew.
Duty takes you; a war must be won,
Good Lord keep you safe from all harm!"

Strange as it may seem to the young, love also happens to older people! In many ways, older lovers find broader meanings and experience deeper relationships. Old eyes often tell stories that are not available to the young, and words are often not necessary. Passions are not so intense, but they are just as sweet! Pleasure can also be achieved by the touch of a hand, a smile, and a quiet moment together. Old eyes still twinkle, and love is good!

Beginnings

Out on the town with you tonight,
Look to the stars, a heavenly sight.
We talk and explore, each other to know,
Future behold, our feelings may grow.

Love seeing you smile, light halos your hair,
I think of tomorrow, things we might share.
Fall of our years, but warmth still remains,
Our hearts are young, we still have dreams.

Enjoy this moment, dwell not the past,
Shape a new future, only love lasts.
Look in my eyes, what do you see?
Do you want a future for two such as we?

No answers now, too early, no guide,
Evenings like this, may help us decide.
Walk with me now, I hold out my hand,
Heal both our hearts, together we stand!

Life is for the living. New relationships mean new promises and expectations. Even for older folk, new beginnings are possible, and love can bloom again!

New Promise

Love is complex; it's hard to explain,
Attachment, passion, refuge from pain.
Kindness and warmth, desire to respond,
Planning and sharing, a will to move on.

Begin a new dream, but remember the old,
The old door closed; a story that's told.
Can't live in sorrow, or bring back the past,
Good memories remain, forever they last.

A promise kept, love 'til life's end,
I must go on, first lover now rests.
New love, God's gift, share and be blessed,
Begin new life, I will ask for your hand.

New promise given, love 'til life's end,
Cherish our moments, broken hearts mend.
I love you and want you, please take my hand,
Bright is our future, love blooms again!

September brings frost; skies are often streaked with gray clouds and the air has a chill. Fall has arrived, and winter will come. Even so, the fall has a certain beauty: leaves are gold, red and brown, the harvest moon shines bright on silver hair, old eyes still twinkle and glow, hearts are still warm, and love arrives on a fall afternoon!

Fall Afternoon

Leaves drift by window, the sun's pale light,
Two seek a future, before winter's night.
A warm caress, two hearts are one,
Love arrives on a fall afternoon.

Gift we are given, to have and to share,
Path may be chosen, to show how we care.
Dark clouds part, time seems to pause,
My heart feels young, you are the cause.

Past cares aside, pain fades away,
What shall we do the rest of our day?
Life isn't over, there's warmth in your eyes.
Can we find peace as leaves drift by?

I know what I see is precious to hold,
Your hand in mine, our story unfolds.
A warm caress, two hearts are one,
Love arrives on a fall afternoon.

Circumstances sometimes require lovers to briefly separate. Jobs, family affairs, and other myriad details of life need our attention; time and distance play their roles. Separation, however brief, causes poignant memories and a longing for the separation to end. We remember the dream gone by and the promise of reunion!

Dream Gone By

Days of laughter, love each night,
We part now, but soon unite.
Hold to memory, our dream gone by,
Vacation's end, we smile and sigh!

Now we'll wait, we'll soon begin,
A life together, 'til days do end.
Begin our future, walk hand in hand,
See the world, this is our plan.

Kiss my love, and gentle touch,
World was ours, enjoyed so much!
We'll part now, but soon enough,
New days of fun, and nights of love!

An evening in a five diamond restaurant provides a wonderful setting for lovers. For most of us, such evenings occur only on very special occasions. The setting, the presentation of the food, the service, and the opportunity to hold hands and gaze into eyes that say so many things: such moments last in our memories long after the evening is done!

An Elegant Room

An elegant room, I'll dine with you,
A harpist plays love's music true.
A magic spell, the tune does weave,
A lover's touch, our hearts believe.

Stars outside, soft silver light,
Comparing pales, your eyes tonight!
Your eyes twinkle, they speak of love,
More than passion, our souls are one.

How can it be, so late, so long?
Find true love and join in song?
We'll walk along our golden path,
Hold my hand, years fly past!

What future holds, I dimly see,
All I ask please walk with me!
Come what may, we'll weather through,
And bravely smile, as lovers must do!

So dine with me, this starry night,
Hear harpist tune, so soft and light.
I hold your hand, and search your eyes,
To find your heart, where love resides!

According to scientists, a pearl is a roundish object produced within the soft tissue of a living shelled mollusk, or clam. A pearl is composed of calcium carbonate in minute crystalline form, deposited in concentric layers. Production of a pearl by a mollusk begins as a defensive response to an irritant such as a parasite or foreign object.

For pearls cultured by man, the foreign object is typically a cut piece of the mollusk's own mantle epithelium, together with a processed piece of shell, the combination of which the mollusk accepts within its soft tissue. The mollusk then begins the process of depositing calcium carbonate around the inserted object. Naturally occurring pearls are common, but rounded gem-quality natural pearls are rare. Cultured pearls are produced in several countries, primarily around the Pacific Rim.

According to poets, a pearl is a luminous, precious thing. Pearls express love, devotion and desire. When a man fastens a string of pearls about a woman's neck, smiles and intimate touches are exchanged. Often, the act of fastening the pearl string is followed with a warm and tender kiss. I prefer the poet's view!

Perfect Pearl

Creamy pearls, lustrous swirls, glowing round and smooth,
On a string, a simple thing, a gift from me to you!
Yet not my gift, but nature's gift, from the tropic seas,
Lowly clams with helping hands grew this gift for thee!

The process known, how they're grown, but add a magic spell,
To make them glow when light is low and lovers touch and tell!
Pearls at rest upon your breast, accent your smile above,
Hold my hand and understand, these pearls express my love!

Walk with me by tropic sea, and know that in the blue,
A special clam at rest in sand holds a gift for you!
A pearl so rare, beyond compare, growing in the deep,
Within my mind search and find this pearl for you to keep!

Look in my eyes, my soul resides, it reaches out to you,
Let our minds soft entwine, and know my love is true!
Deeper still, find you will, perfect, round and smooth,
A dreamy pearl, growing still, a lover's gift for you!

During a recent visit to the Big Island of Hawaii, my wife and I enjoyed a suite at the Fairmont Orchid. The lanai just off the bedroom had a stunning view across the beach and out over the Pacific Ocean. Early mornings provided an especially inviting ambiance; even now, after our return home, I can see the pale silver light, feel the soft breezes and hear the sound of surf!

During our stay at the Orchid, I usually got up early; old habits are hard to break. I would then dress in a light robe, make a pot of coffee, stand by the rail on the lanai and for a few minutes, sip coffee while my wife slept. Such moments were meant for daydreams and for composing the following poem!

Ocean Blue

Ocean blue, endless view, soft silver morning glow,
You still sleep, dream so deep, I watch the sea tide flow!
From lanai, hear palm trees sigh, hot coffee in my cup,
Begin my day a quiet way, you stir but not yet up!

Back inside, dim room light, I turn from ocean blue,
Eyes perceive a scene to please, my gaze envelopes you!
Your tousled hair, face so fair, curves in silken clothes,
'Neath lace so light, heart's delight, every nuance shows!

Hear the surf, swirling 'round, formed from ocean blue,
Heart keeps time, nature's rhyme; glide through door to you!
Return to bed, no words said, you smile though eyes stay closed,
Lightly touch, desire so much, my arms 'round you enfold!

Sunrise bold, room turns gold; the tide does ebb and flow,
Together seek emotions peak, then peace that lovers know!
Through open door soft breezes flow, palm trees gently sigh,
In bed we lay while sunbeams play, bright from morning sky!

Late we rise, adjust our eyes to light from waiting sun,
Meet the day a timeless way, the tide has ebbed and run!
View the scene, earth so green, meets the surf line white,
Then ocean blue, endless view, it flows beyond our sight!

Just hold my hand, here we stand, to talk and plan our day,
We'll seek and find peace of mind, a place where lovers play!
Perhaps the view of ocean blue along the sea tide flow,
Will bring the joy that lovers seek, a path in golden glow!

Hawaii hosts many beautiful orchids: white, lavender, pink, yellow, pastels, an endless variety of mixed colors and so on. The orchid family includes over twenty-two thousand species; a large number of these lovely creations grace Hawaii's gardens and parklands.

Almost all of the orchids in Hawaii were brought in by man. Over many generations, the hands of man guided the development of beautiful orchid flowers into hybrids that please the eye and sooth the soul.

Someday, if you can, walk in a Hawaiian garden. More often than not, early in the morning, just before sunrise, doves will coo softly in the shadows; small colorful birds will flit through the trees, and water will tinkle through unseen rivulets under the dense foliage. Perhaps you will spy a white orchid flower, soft, fragile, beautiful, resting among green leaves, waiting just for you!

Dream Flower

Orchid white, morning light, at rest in garden green,
Perfect flower, magic power: so smooth, untouched, pristine!
A soul at rest with nature's best: let greater world endure,
Contemplate, cares can wait, see flower so white and pure!

Hybrid flower, nature's power, yet thoughts control the scene,
Swirling whorls, shapely curls, 'round a central theme!
Broad white sepals, small pink petals, pastel colored veins,
Attracts your eye, like insects fly, 'round and 'round again!

My flower has more, an open door, find the dreams within,
Like pollen dust, dreams for us, spread softly on the wind!
Fragile things pollen dreams, your flower is now required,
Dreams may rest in your soft nest and form the seed desired!

My orchid flower has dreamer's power, create and then give way,
Essence share my dreams so fair, new thoughts for each new day!
Your flower waits for breeze and fates; to touch and then move on,
Perchance you'll sleep, my dreams you'll keep, nature's plan be done!

Dreams so soft, they rise aloft, spread through air so clear,
White orchid dreams, thoughts serene, to rest with you my dear!
Your heart knows a seed will grow, your flower so white on green,
Just seek the wind and new begin: so smooth, untouched, pristine!

Most dreamers go to special places to find emotional insight and answers to life's questions. I often go to such places. Sometimes I go during the light of day. More often I go at night. Imagine: the house is quiet, everyone sleeps, and insight and answers are just a dream away! My mind roams free, it must be said; I dream a lot, when I'm in bed!

River Song

High mountain valley, under azure-blue sky,
Just one dream away and dreamers can fly!
Clear swift water, from crystal white snows,
Feeds valley river; soft silver light glows!
Ripples make melody, as water moves on,
Breeze provides base, to swift river song!
So silent I wait, while water sweet sings,
Music takes form, from tinkles and pings!

A vision arrives, by swift silver water,
Radiant beauty, see cold river's daughter!
In sparkling sunlight, from blue sky above,
Contrast to cold, her voice speaks of love!
I intently observe; true meaning I'll find,
Feeling her words, my emotions refined!
Music and vision, both timeless yet new,
Wise river daughter, she tells me of you!

Soft singing voice, the sound is divine,
Meaning is clear, to search and to find!
River's sweet daughter, points to a way,
A path now revealed; it winds past today!
On it leads, from today through tomorrow,
Follow her guidance, leave today's sorrow!
So silent I wait, while the river voice sings,
Vision surrounds mid tinkles and pings!

Time to leave valley, dreamer turns home,
Refreshed and rested, my mind holds a poem!
Found rhymes to describe, my vision by water,
Words to enlighten, from swift river's daughter!
She pointed the way, you wait just ahead,
Decision was made, words have been said!
Rise from my dream, swift water still sings,
My vision found, mid tinkles and pings!

When you go to bed at night, do you occasionally dream and somehow know that your lover shares the same dream? I do! Confirmation comes in the morning in the form of your lover's knowing smile!

Dreams

When evening comes I'll do my best,
To be at peace and drift to rest.
And though I sleep I true believe,
That as I dream, you dream with me.

To magic land our souls will go,
Greet gentle people, sing soft and low.
By Crystal Lake, walk hand in hand,
A quiet place, with pure white sand.

The evening sun dips in the mist,
Watch it glow, and tender kiss.
The stars appear and moon on high,
The lake all silver, the breeze soft sigh.

You're dressed in white, with satin shoes,
I'm dressed in blue, with golden hues.
And though we sleep, I still believe,
That in our dream, you walk with me.

Even after new beginnings, there are somber moments. Memories come to the foreground, especially when a person is alone, the house is quiet, and firelight flickers on the hearth.

Memories

I sit beside the fire and think of my lover's warmth and glow,
The dancing light upon her hair that I always cherished so.

I sit in quiet somber dream, of times that might have been,
Now listen for returning feet and her voice beyond the door.

For that door is there for me; sometimes I pray and often dream,
I shall pass, forever see, my lover's smile and welcome hand!

My first lover rests in Heaven now, in a place with many beautiful flowers. I think about her every day.

Life goes on. I have met and married a wonderful lady and opened a new chapter. I am truly blessed because I have been and continue to be loved by two very special ladies. I know my first wife smiles and wishes joy to those who live.

Sonnets provide a wonderful way to express love and longing. Shakespeare did it best. Even across a span of over four hundred years, his sonnets inspire so many people to believe in the enduring power of love! The following two original poems draw upon, but do not copy, Shakespeare's inspiring work. Notice that each poem carries two main ideas (octave and sestet), and weaves them into one fabric. Enjoy!

Time's Mirror

My mirror shall not persuade me that I grow old;
So long as youth and you both share one date,
But when time's furrows I upon my brow behold,
I will turn toward you and see beauty in my fate!
Time will not draw lines on my fair lover's brow;
Nor blemish her smooth face now so loving fair,
Let her always be as I remember here and now,
My love shall live on in verse; time shall not care!
Let time do whatever time should do in flowing;
And show new seasons as through clearest glass,
I ask only that time pass my love by unknowing!
Yet it is my best wish my lover will not long pass;
Over time and seasons to share her love and fate,
For my waiting heart now offers love an open gate!

Enduring Beauty

Relentless time, please soften passion's mood;
And let your long days dry up my lover's tears,
Take the sting from fierce and careless words,
And then assuage her deepest hurts and fears!
Let time preserve her soft beauty deep within;
And continue heart's warmth in complex ways,
Let love's welcome patterns in her heart begin,
And love augment her beauty for all future days!
In spite of time and world and all the seasons past;
We share all that life presents and can be endured,
We shall brave the seasons and bold time's repast,
From now until life's end, and then to rest assured,
That heaven will continue what we on earth do cast,
And beyond that gate forever provide a golden path!

Shakespeare's sonnets (and the above pale imitations) always seem so serious! According to the Bard, love becomes an almost painful longing, with a strong dose of wishful dreaming! Let's have some fun, and pretend that it's springtime, and the critters are all a-doin' it! Even the muskrats are splishin', splashin', feelin' passion!

Consider the following "sonnet," and note the variation in meter from the "pure" form.

Springtime Lovin'

Springtime, springtime, days so fair, time for passion, love to share;
The squirrels a-chasin', the rabbits racin', all runnin' wild and free,
Now chase that tail! O'er hill and dale! Try an' catch that gal so fair,
All the critters know; their hearts a-glow; now what 'bout you an' me?
The insects a-buzzin', the pollen's blowin', trees turn green right soon;
And blossoms poppin', frogs all hoppin', an' swimmin' 'round in glee,

Muskrat passion, splish an' splashin', they're a -squeakin' at the moon,
And the foxes jumpin', somethin's pumpin; now what 'bout you an' me?
All the critters show, what we should know, "bout springtime love an' fun;
Nature's way for sayin' it's time for playin'! Let's set our passions free,
Just spin all 'round, jump up an' down, like squirrels chase tail an' run,
Let's let it flow, so hearts will glow; now please will you chase with me?
Springtime, fun-time, our days of glee, let's get down an' have our spree,
It's your tail I'm chasin'! Stop that racin'! I'll catch you, wait an' see!

Sometimes in my autumn years, the myriad details of daily life fade from view. In the evening sky or in the soft lamplight glow, I see visions. Past, present, and future mix and swirl around me. Alternative paths become visible, and consequences of choice among the many paths become apparent. I also review old visions, and I am content with what I see!

Sweetheart Dream!

That old dream of mine! I sense its presence here with me,
And it's not just a vain creation of an old lover's memory!
It was a fair and illusive vision, that came so long ago,
I didn't even cause it; it came on an evening glow!

Yet I true believed it; it came from heaven's light so true,
The vision was of future love, now substance here with you!
The then before so many days and the now of autumn time,
Your love o'er years was smiling, oh present sweetheart mine!

The ever sense of knowing, though long years did intervene,
With times of work and growing, old pictures tell the scene!
I saw you then as you are now, your love a constant theme,
You waited for the moment when fate made real the dream!

Sometimes at home when I'm alone I muse on what we dare,
Then in my mind I seek and find the meaning in all we share!
So in the light of my old dreams, I perceive the great design,
I see the path, our golden path, with you, oh Sweetheart mine!

Sometimes the lamplight glimmers, there's a flicker of surprise,
Then I turn low the lamplight glow to rest the dazzle in my eyes!
And I see the night in silence, full of stars and the silver moon,
They shine softly through my window, past shadows in the room!

It's my time for introspection, for loving thoughts that start,
Like moonlight glow and starlight show, illuminate my heart!
Then I recall my dream of long ago, a luxury so sweet divine,
And on golden path I wander, with you, oh Sweetheart mine!

But ah! My dream is broken, by a presence soft and fair,
The door is slowly opened, and you are standing there!
Then with eager heart enraptured, all my visions I resign,
To greet your living presence, oh you Sweetheart mine!

Now we plan our journey, in our quiet evening spot,
Our days of wine and roses, be thankful for our lot!
And then we'll share the old vision fair, and kiss so tenderly,
Angels smile in heaven, now that you're down here with me!

3. DISNEY WORLD

Disney World has much more than just the best theme parks in the world. It has themed luxury resorts, five-diamond fine dining, beautiful golf courses, and a fantastic array of parades, theaters, spas, dancing, lounges, stores and nightclubs. You name it and if it provides good, wholesome family fun; Disney probably has it!

Disney World is not just for kids; "old folks" can have great time too! No wonder that Disney World hosts millions of excited families, lovers, and seniors each year. Everyone can leave cares and frustrations at the gate, walk in, and experience the magic!

My wife and I, our children, and my grandchildren have spent many wonderful moments in Disney World. In this chapter, we will take a "park hopping" approach to Walt's special domain. Before each poem, I will give you a "heads up" on where we are at the moment. We will start with one of our favorite Disney resorts. If you want a methodical approach to touring Disney, buy a guidebook!

When we were young, we vacationed at the "World" on a shoestring budget. Now that we are older and can afford elegant vacations, we go to the luxury resorts. We were poor, now we are affluent. I like being affluent better! For us, the romantic side of Disney World begins at the Grand Floridian!

The Grand

Grand Resort, in sandy cove fair,
Pools and fountains, meticulous care!
Gables and turrets, fresh flowers delight,
Roof deep red, walls gleaming white!

Approach by land or quaint little boat,
A sparkling scene, take special note.
Welcoming hands, fresh smiling faces,
Greetings in style, old southern graces.

Fluffy white clouds, blue azure sky,
Seagulls and ospreys sail effortlessly by.
Pixie dust floats down from above,
Walt is proud, a labor of love!

Castle in distance, bathed in pale light,
Enjoy quiet evening, fireworks delight!
Time for bed, children to sleep,
Adults watch stars, black velvet deep.

Wake in the morning, big doin's today!
Mickey just called, get ready to play!
Dew on the roses and manicured lawn,
Robins in trees, singing since dawn.

Stroll down to breakfast, coffee and tea,
Fresh juice and cake, just wait and see!
Children excited, hardly can wait,
Soon after breakfast, run to the gate!

Monorail glides slow to a stop,
Open the gate, park hoppers hop!
Glide down the track, path in the sky,
Parks in the distance, to them we fly!

A magical day, glide back in style,
Return to the Grand, tired with a smile.
Back to our room, sleep sound tonight,
Tomorrow's awaitin', new magic delight!

Grand is special, see smiling faces,
Care with style, old southern graces.
Once we arrived, the world went away,
Enjoyed the magic, the length of our stay!

No matter how many times we visit the Walt's Magic Kingdom, we are awed by its beauty and attention to detail. Some folks think of the "Kingdom" in terms of attractions and rides, parades and fireworks, but the Kingdom is truly magical!

Main Street, just inside the gate, provides a good example. Remember small towns and summer evenings? When I was a boy, I often walked with my father, grandmother and sister just six blocks from our home to downtown on Main Street in Clinton, Indiana. It was a time before television, telephones were scarce, and computers did not exist. Model A Ford cars and even a few horses were on the streets!

Those times are now just a memory. However, we can get a glimpse of those times, just a glimpse mind you, on Main Street within the Magic Kingdom. Do you remember?

Main Street

Walkin' down town, Main Street the way,
Find magic lands, and castle so gay!
Shops each side, neat mercantile stash,
Thousands of ways, spend all your cash!

Yet special it is, recall yesteryear,
Small town street, memories still dear.
See in our minds, time of our youth,
Main Street lived, sparkling and new!

Time changes all, hard now to find,
Places like memories, frozen in time.
Only an image, best we can see,
Yet it refreshes, gold memories to me!

Young folk laugh, quaint buildings and such,
They miss the point, Walt's loving touch.
Walt made it special, old folks smile,
Tears wash memories, be wistful awhile!

Slowly to castle, savor the time,
Block out noises, old memories refine,
Hear sounds that drift, down from above,
Laughter and streetcars, sounds that we love!

Horses clip-clopping, vendors chant low,
Memories we have, from long long ago.
Walkin' down town, Main Street the way,
Long long ago? Seems yesterday!

Fantasyland in the Kingdom hosts the "Winnie the Pooh" ride. Kids love it. So do adults, even if they don't want to admit it. Kids ooh! and aah! over the antics of Winnie and his friends. Adults smile and their eyes twinkle as they pass through the doors in their

"Hunny Pot;" they magically become children again!

Winnie the Pooh

Tigger and Piglet, bear with a Pooh,
Start gentle adventure, a pleasant to-do!
One hundred acres, condensed in a ride,
Adults all smile, children's eyes wide!

Hold tight my hand, climb pot inside,
Winnie and friends play while we ride.
Glide through the wood, spin slowly 'round,
Pink hefalumps stare, blue woozles abound!

There goes Kanga, Roo in a pouch,
Eyore looks mournful, Rabbit a grouch!
Owl sounds wise, but really is not,
Chris Robin solves problems, explores every plot!

Adventure time ends, glide to a stop,
Lift up the rail, touch gold hunny pot.
Look through the stuff, Pooh's Thotful Shop,
Say 'bye to Pooh, no time to stop!

Now for a change of pace: let's leave the Kingdom, take a ride on the Disney Monorail (with a change of trains at the Ticket and Transportations Center), and head on over to Walt's Experimental Prototype City of Tomorrow, or EPCOT. Don't worry; we will come back to the Kingdom a little later!

EPCOT has many attractions that excite and impress. However, there are also a few places where adults can reflect and muse over simple things; nothing deep or complicated mind you, just quiet reflections.

The Coral Reef Restaurant is such a place. Fish swim by in a huge glass aquarium, and diners sit at comfortable tables in the dim light, watching the fish.

By Coral Sea

This quiet day, I'll dine with you,
By Coral Sea, where light shines through.
Fish swim by, slow and smooth,
Their eyes stare, from shadows blue.

They must know, we also see,
From darkened room, in silent dream.
We contemplate, we wonder why,
Will answers come, as fish swim by?

Do they know we live and love?
In separate world, on land above?
See their eyes? They seem to show,
Secret ways that we should know.

Mysterious world, this Coral Sea,
Silent depths, life's meaning seek.
Do fish know, how I feel?
New passion glow, old wounds heal?

Thoughts I beam, in shadows blue,
Let them know, my soul seeks truth.
No answers come, just fishy stares,
Separate worlds, and different cares.

I'll turn to you, for I must know,
Your eyes will tell; they twinkle so!
Hold my hand, look in my eyes,
Know my heart, where love resides!

One evening some time ago, I walked alone in the garden behind the British Pavilion at EPCOT. I mused quietly as I strolled along. I was looking forward to meeting a certain wonderful lady the very next day at the Grand Floridian. We had plans to spend five days together at Disney World. I could see that love was in my future, and I was happier than I had been in a very long time. It was a warm evening, and the sun was setting behind the trees at the edge of the garden.

To my surprise, Mary Poppins stepped out from one of the British Pavilion buildings! She walked past several other people and strolled straight up to me! I knew she was an actress playing a part of course, but somehow, it seemed more. Mary (the actress) had a knowing way of looking at me, and she had a twinkle in her eyes!

Mary's Promise

Met Mary Poppins, dressed red and white,
Angelic her smile, a lovely sight!
Prim and proper, yet wondrously kind,
Offered my hand, she didn't mind.

Words she gave and set me at ease,
Kindled my hopes, like soft summer breeze.
Breeze rippled roses, touched my gray hair,
Told me of love, in autumn so fair!

Golden sunrise, you'll hold my hand,
Mary's smile told me, in magical land!
Mary took leave in her special way,
She gave me hope for a sun-filled day!

Bright future awaits, soon we shall wed,
Autumn sees blossoms, fall roses so red.
Mary assured me, you I will see,
Tomorrow in garden, lovers we'll be!

There is a wonderful end to this little "Mary Poppins" story. Five months to the day after meeting and talking with Mary at EPCOT, the lady that met me at the Grand Floridian became my wife. We were married at the Grand Floridian on July 25, 2007!

Now back to the Kingdom! Since my wife Linda and I are relative newlyweds, we find the old train especially romantic!

To Linda: In the past, I rode the old steam train all around the park. I have good memories. Now, I look forward to a new ride with you! Familiar places, old and new faces, train circles around, new love we've found! Old Disney train, but ride is new; you're now by my side; enjoy the view!

Magic Train

At Disney's main station, let's board the train,
Again ride the circle, love's familiar refrain!
A choice at the station, leave town and the past,
Soft scenery abounds, add memories that last!
Hear clickety clack, the rails make a sound,
With you by my side, as we ride all around!
I've been here before, but somehow it's new,
Welcome the difference, to circle with you!

Old magic train, big wheels turn around,
It huffs and puffs, a familiar soft sound!
Hearts now sing, like train bell's clear ring,
Engineer swings it, swing ring, ding ding!
Please hold my hand; our vows have been made,
Time for our journey, we'll glide through the glade!
I've been here before, but gold sunset's our view,
Content with the difference, to circle with you!

Happy old train, rails simple and sure,
Gently it sways, our love feels secure!
Warm next to you, to travel we're bound,
Finding new joys; as train circles 'round!
My eyes they twinkle; you give me a smile,
See pretty sights? We'll enjoy every mile!
I've been here before, the signposts are here,
We are the difference, just you and me dear!

Familiar old train, we both know its sound,
Soft, gentle smooth, as we circle around!
Gray hair ruffles, warm breezes we feel,
Touches our faces; old wounds gently heal!
Kisses are sweet; they're better with age,
Ride to our sunset; then turn the next page!
I've been here before, but the ride feels new,
Loving the difference, sharing with you!

From Mickey's sorcerer's hat to the Tower of Terror, Disney Hollywood Studios (formerly Disney-MGM Studios) presents a "fantasmic" array of attractions! So let's "park hop" again and head on over!

The charming Muppets were created by Jim Henson and company in the mid 1950s. Beginning in 1969, they gained worldwide fame on the long running TV show: "Sesame Street." Numerous Muppet movies and TV appearances followed. The Muppets under the Jim Henson Company opened their pavilion at Disney World in the early 1990s, and key portions of the Company were purchased by the Walt Disney Company in 2004.

For over two decades, the Muppet characters at Disney World have brought wry humor and much laughter to millions of children as well as adults, who, for awhile, want to be children again! Read the poem and imagine the Disney Muppet Show!

Muppets!

Muppets are puppets, let fantasy take flight,
Play-toys that act, just smile with delight!
Muppet Three-D, you'll jump with surprise,
Kermit's the leader; he's green and eats flies!

Penguins at pre-show, theme music they play,
Sam Eagle takes charge, but penguins want pay!
Nothing goes right, poor Sam's at a loss,
Kermit stays calm, good thing he's boss!

Bad jokes from Fozzie, a bear with cream pies,
He throws 'um we dodge 'um, just close your eyes!
Statler and Waldorf, just ornery old men,
Puppets that heckle, poor Fozzie can't win!

Then Bunsen and Beaker, Muppet lab goes awry,
Experiment on Beaker, poor Beaker! Oh my!
Then somehow a chef, wild gibberish he speakish,
Kitchen be-witchin' smorgasboardin' in Swedish!

Then Piggy's the star, just ask her you'll see,
A pig with a wig, sex symbol times three!
Miss Piggy sings, just slightly off-key,
Romantic the setting, a pig by a tree!

Bunny tries helping, pig temper grows hotter,
Song turns to scream, a pig under water!
Poor Bunny's so funny, tried hard to be helpful,
He then runs away, best efforts were doubtful!

Sweetum jumps out, wild, crazy yet funny,
Runs all around, then searches for Bunny!
Bunny gets found, after search high and low,
Kermit's relieved; then winds up the show!

Slapstick but fun, just nonsense unbound,
Believe in magic, when Muppets are 'round!
Muppets are puppets, hearts they do steal,
Play-toys that act, yet somehow they're real!

Now back to the Kingdom! The "Pirates of the Caribbean" attraction is on every visitor's "to do" list. Never mind what a pirate's life was really like, this Disney version is pure family fun! Let's all be pirates, Disney style!

Pirates!

Avast ye Swabs! Scurvy crew waits!
Caution to winds! Trust to our fates!
Buckle your swash, ready for sea,
Sail Spanish Main, pirates we'll be!

See Capt'n Jack, struttin' on deck?
Eyes darkly gleam, havoc he'll wreak!
Borderline swishy, but ladies' heartthrob,
Charming young scoundrel, treasures he'll rob!

Capt'n Jack's ship, port we'll arrive,
Rescue fair lady, from castle so high.
Forced to marry, heartbroken she be,
Jack makes escape, freedom at sea!

Lovin' and scrappin', pirate's fair match,
Lady on board, batten the hatch!
She swings a cutlass, fights with the best,
She gives poor Jack, so little earned rest!

Rove the broad sea, fear not the gales,
But Davy Jones waits, ghost ship he sails!
Fight for our lives! Ghost cannons blow!
Davy may win, his realm we must go!

Slimy old faces and skeletons grim,
Await dead sailors, sea floor so dim!
But Davy must heed, curse works both ways,
Signed foc'sle contract, treasure's been paid!

From sea bottom up, see light of day!
Ghosts can't follow, so anchors aweigh!
Off to sunrise, sail as we please,
Gold seekers hunt, across the broad sea!

Now you've heard, my rollicking tale,
Lovin' and fightin', stormy winds gale!
So buckle your swash, make ready for sea,
Sail with bold Jack, and pirates we'll be!

Hot summer evenings and ice cream go together. Add a little hot fudge and you experience a delight straight from Heaven! I know just the place, and it's in Downtown Disney!

Ghirardelli's

Right from a fountain, chocolate ice cream,
Special for you, vacation time dream.
No calories please, but everything else,
Sprinkles on top, don't let it melt!

Walked all day, in Florida heat,
Lost several pounds, earned a sweet treat!
With calories out, no guilt will appear,
Savor each bite, contentment my dear!

Two spoons, one treat, show me you care,
Down to last bites, think we can share?
Only for you, I'll lower my spoon,
Buy more ice cream, soon as we're through!

Finally we finish, add tummy spread,
Planned only one, bought two treats instead.
Calories found us, they slipped right down,
We'll walk off pounds, through Disney Downtown!

Combine a zoo and a theme park, and what do you get? Disney's Animal Kingdom of course! Every bug, tiger, crocodile, eagle and gorilla is in its proper place, and they pose no danger to the tourists. Even the local mosquitoes have been told they cannot bite.

The only danger that I know of are the kids; one of them may drop an ice cream cone on your foot as you walk by (it happened to me once). Otherwise you will be perfectly safe!

Animals Alive!

Animal Kingdom's the place to be,
Giraffes and bugs and others to see!
Elephants, tigers, and birds on the wing,
Bats and rats, and Lion the King!

Walk through the trees, cross over bridge,
See sleek otters, by dark river's edge?
Carved tree of life, look closely you'll see,
All kinds of faces, staring at thee!

Safari old trucks, rattle all 'round,
Out on savannah, see zebras they bound?
Antelope graze, just chewing their cud,
Little Red's venture, go play in the mud!

Stroll Pangani Trail, gorillas in mist,
Looking at us, how 'bout a kiss?
They play all day or sleep as they please,
Who's really smarter, gorillas or me?

See ruined temple, eyes staring out,
A tiger appears, all striped about!
Glad he's there and we're over here,
Invites us to lunch, entrée my dear!

Walk around park, to Dinosaur Land,
A scary adventure, but know it's pretend!
Now time for lunch, we've walked all about,
Find African town, seek Tusker House!

Lunch in the shade, listen to songs,
African music, keep time with the drums!
Afternoon passes, fill in the gaps,
Shops full of stuff, trade for our cash!

On the way out, look at the vine,
It crawls on a wall, creepy eyes shine!
Watch a parade, floats Mickey built,
Outlandish costumes, people on stilts!

Happy but tired, hurry to bus,
Ride to resort, kids make a fuss.
Finally to room, glad we're back,
Watch pretty sunset, then hit the sack!

EPCOT defies any attempt at a simple description. It is my favorite Disney theme park. It entertains and educates; it treats guests to spectacular fireworks and laser shows; it provides a showcase for many cultures from around the world, it – well, just go see it!

Experimental Prototype City of Tomorrow (EPCOT)

EPCOT today, see white sphere so high,
Monorail circles, path in the sky!
Future awaits, thrill rides galore,
Country pavilions, so much in store!

Comm and transport, energy to burn,
Land, sea and fountain, so much to learn!
Inventions and space, eyes wide with awe,
Physical science, great Universe law!

See beyond fountain, pavilions await,
Cross over bridge, past International Gate.
France and Great Britain, and Italy too,
China and Nippon, Morocco so new!

Viking's surprise and Deutschland so quaint,
Mexican scenes, then walk 'round the lake.
American story and Canadian steak,
Buy souvenirs, soft drinks and cake!

So much to see, so much to do,
EPCOT to be, but thinking of you!
Fireworks and lasers light up the night,
End perfect day, and children's delight!

"La Nouba" in Downtown Disney is not a circus, even though it has clowns, trapeze artists, acrobats, jugglers and high wire walkers. It is not a musical, even though it has talented singers and spectacular choreography. It is not a stage show, even though it has production numbers and wonderful special effects. It is just, well, special and unique!

La Nouba!

Cirque du Soleil in Disney Downtown,
Amazing performers, funny old clowns!
High show La Nouba, talent so rare,
Nothing I've seen could ever compare!

Trapeze and jugglers, dancers go 'round,
Acrobats tumble, bouncy, bound bound!
Colors and swirls, high in the air,
Bicycles jump, wire walkers dare!

Spin like a top, balance and poise,
Lights flash and glow, magical toys!
Look to the ceiling, fly with such ease,
Follow and twirl, split timing trapeze!

Vibrant songs, echo and flow,
Beautiful voices, wonder to know!
Mind in a whirl, spinning all 'round,
See awesome people, match musical sound!

High show La Nouba, talent so rare,
Wonders and colors, artists who dare!
Imagine and dream, the story unfolds,
To memory send, moments in gold!

My family and I have been to Disney World many times, and we don't even live in Florida! Each time we find new things to do; we hate to leave, and we look forward to the next visit. Magic truly comes alive at Disney World, and no, I am not on Disney's payroll!

Magical Land

Fly to the sun, our chariot waits,
Days of delight and dizzy new heights!
A place that teems with sparkling streams,
See gentle people, together we dream!

Once we enter, cares melt away,
Time stands still, the length of our stay.
Chocolate treats, fireworks displays,
Boat rides and beaches, children at play!

Lions and tigers stroll peacefully by,
Birds always sing; trees come alive!
Sunshine above, walk hand in hand,
Sharing and laughing, in magical land!

Sunshine is free, white clouds we'll see,
Air will be fresh, warm breezes will please.
I need only you, in this happy land,
Make life complete, please take my hand!

Lights, cameras, action and happy holidays! Christmas, Disney style, is special and unique. The parks and resorts are crowded; kids, with parents in tow, fill every nook and cranny. It's wall to wall people at every attraction and in every restaurant. Yet, in spite of the crowds, the experience is worth a few minor inconveniences. Just go!

Disney Christmas!

Let's join the Disney party, Mickey's full of cheer,
He sings a Yuletide carol and welcomes friends so dear!
Minnie giggles, Donald wiggles, Goofy sings along,
Let your heart be joyful, hear the season's song!
Disney Christmas special, there's magic in the air,
Remember why we celebrate; end your worldly care!

Walk around the castle, see changing colored light,
Anticipate; pass the gate, fireworks sparkle bright!
Hold my hand; stroll along, down the crowded street,
See the toys, children's joys, arranged so prim and neat!
Sparkling lights and angels, there's magic in the air,
Reminds us why we celebrate, the gift we all do share!

Look up my dear, see crystals clear, dancing through the sky,
Snow and love float from above, against the night they fly!
Fake snow we know; in the glow, it lands on tropic leaves,
But end your doubt; turn about, like children true believe!
Leave the park, stroll down the walk, there's magic in the air,
Remember why we celebrate, a love so true and fair!

Walk to the lake, a boat awaits, see it slowly docking,
Helping hand to board from land, the boat is gently rocking!
Look back to shore, yes there's more, Mickey waves goodbye,
It's make believe but sure to please, smile and wistful sigh!
Kingdom fair fades from view, yet magic's in the air,
Christmas love we celebrate, a joy we gladly share!

Out we go, gliding slow, across the moonlit lake,
To Grand Resort, look to port, silver in our wake!
Feel the breeze, our hair to tease, sit and huddle near,
Warm you are next to me; I love you true my dear!
You make my Christmas special, there's magic in the air,
Remember dear we celebrate, God's gift so true and fair!

Linda: Remember the Osborne Family lights at Disney Hollywood Studios? An enchanting moment; you smiled, and time stood still!

Osborne Family Lights

Anticipate, great joy awaits, deep in Christmas dark,
Distant glow, golden flow, from across the Disney Park!
Smiling faces from distant places, all have gathered here,
To walk in peace, all strife to cease, this special time of year!
Across the square, Mickey's there! Let your dreams take flight,
See Christmas scene, how it gleams, with Osborne Family lights!

Six million lights, they shine so bright, along the cobbled street,
We walk along; hear season's song, and smile to all we meet!
High in the sky, angels fly! They soar upon the heights,
Trumpets sound and all around, glorious dancing lights!
Around the square, children stare, magic dreams take flight,
Snow crystals gleam, faces beam, in Osborne Family lights!

Glad we're here, you see my dear, love we've truly found,
Hand in hand, here we stand, and lights glow all around!
Hearts rejoice, we've made our choice, now it's time to play,
From deep within we're young again, although our hair is gray!
Christmas time, the bells all chime, magic dreams take flight,
Survey the scene, how they gleam, the Osborne Family lights!

Time does pause, see Santa Claus! He speaks to us my dear,
It's not pretend; his voice does send a message soft but clear!
Now all must know here below; just see and true believe,
Christmas love comes from above, God's great gift receive!
Six million lights glow so bright, let your dreams take flight,
A Christmas scene, how it gleams, with Osborne Family lights!

In the Kingdom, a brooding, spooky old mansion sits on an isolated hillside between

Liberty Square and Fantasy Land. It's Disney World at its best, and it's haunted! Technically, the Haunted Mansion is one of the Liberty Square attractions. However, its spirit (pun intended) is more in tune with Fantasy Land. The mansion experience is more fun than scary; but what the heck, let's be children again!

Haunted Mansion!

Hold my hand, it's Fantasy Land! Believe and walk right in,
Find mansion grand, let's pretend, that ghosts reside therein!
Hear ravens cry, sad spirits sigh; graves brood on the hill,
Pass black gate, resign your fate; wind wafts damp and chill!

Spooky room, scream of doom! Join the frightened throng,
It's now too late! Doom buggy waits! Hear the eerie song!
Bold eyes peer out, from walls about, cobwebs either side,
Bar drops down, locked all round! Start the mansion ride!

Pass banquet hall, a ghostly ball! Song beats three-fourths time,
Spooks are loose; not Mother Goose! Chills run down your spine!
A talking head, hear what's said! A heart goes thump-a-thump,
Black spiders spin; ghosts all grin; spooks go jump and bump!

Ghosts a-wavin' too late for savin'! They sit beside and ride,
Then bar pops up, time to jump, from buggy to moving side!
The end of tour, find the door! We may come back someday,
Just to look, like a storybook, we sure don't want to stay!

Sprint to gate, it's not our fate, to reside upon this hill,
Find sunlight, warm and bright, leave the damp and chill!
Mansion grand, we did pretend; ghosts roam halls therein,
Hold my hand, leave Fantasy Land, smile, and understand!

Some Disney rides are timeless. They appeal to the kid in each of us. "Dumbo" in the Kingdom is one of these. The basic design is nearly one hundred years old. It consists of a complex mechanical wheel with spokes that move up then down as the wheel gently spins around. The basic design can be found at almost any county fair midway. Disney just added a "Dumbo" flying elephant at the end of each spoke for each set of passengers instead of "cars" or other cartoon-like vehicles found at county fairs. The ride time is less than three minutes.

For many older adults, the Dumbo ride brings golden memories to the fore. Remember "The Wonderful World of Disney" TV program? In the mid 1950s, this black and white TV show was a Sunday night ritual for many kids. We would park in front of the TV set in pajamas. Mom and Dad would move around in the background doing whatever adults did in those days. At seven PM, the music would start; Tinker Bell would do her thing and open the "Disneyland" curtain, and the opening scenes on the TV would be quick snippets of the fabulous Disneyland Park! Prominent in the opening would be a view of kids on the Dumbo ride! The scene would fade to Walt Disney. Walt would then do his monologue to introduce the evening program. Somehow, standing in line for the Dumbo ride at Disney World brings it all back; it is one of Walt's original rides. Golden memories!

At the Kingdom, kids with adults in tow line up for Dumbo. Often, they wait over an hour for a three minute ride. Few complain. Afterwards, nearly every passenger wears a grin as they walk away, even adults. Wasn't that fun!? Maybe it was the Pixie dust!

Dumbo

Walk around the Toontown, where Mickey Mouse resides,
Past Small World and Teacups, and a dozen other rides!
Just find a ride so simple, a gold memory trip behold,
It's a ring of flying elephants, a joy for young and old!
Long lines they're always waitin', kids with folks in tow,
Dumbo lands; people load; then round and round they go!
Dumbo up; Dumbo down; watch the park sail by,
Laugh with glee; fly with me, on Dumbo in the sky!

On every trip to Disney, some rides just can't be missed,
Don't know why elephants fly, but Dumbo's on our list!
Just wait in line for cycle time, three minutes in the air,
Dumbo's flight is nearly like the rides at county fair!
But Disney made it special; they add a magic touch,
Maybe Pixie dust or somethin', we all enjoy so much!
A familiar thing that tugs heart strings, Dumbo sets us free,
I'm on a spree, the kid in me, just feel the summer breeze!

So when you walk to Toontown, see Mickey with his friends,
Then continue on, hum a song, find Dumbo's ride again!
The line winds 'round and 'round, patient wait worthwhile,
See all the kids anticipatin', to greet Dumbo's happy smile!
See adult eyes all a- twinkle; they can't suppress a grin,
Just climb aboard and hold my hand; let the fun begin!
Dumbo up; Dumbo down; watch laughing kids fly by,
They're wild and free, just like me, with Dumbo in the sky!

Back to EPCOT! Fast cars, squealing tires, roaring engines, hand and power tools in fantastic machine shops, test dummies and other smashing things that go bang! You have arrived at Disney's Test Track!

Sponsored by General Motors, the Test Track at EPCOT provides marvelous fun for kids, teenagers, and especially for old men who think they are still teenagers. Remember tinkering with your first car when you were sixteen? Wouldn't it be wonderful to have had a machine shop like the one at Disney's Test Track? Wow!

Test Track!

Hear the roar? Yes there's more! Across the EPCOT Park,
High fun waits, fast pass gates, a Test Track in the dark!
Line winds round, hear that sound? Click and clack and smack,
Test dummies stare, just over there, smash and crash and crack!
Don't be dummy, won't be funny, don't smash and break apart,
Lesson there, seat belts wear, with speed be safe and smart!
Line moves down, cars come round, six per car each load,
Are you ready? Just hold steady! It's time to hit the road!

Quick check TV, tests to see, expect a scary ride,
First anti-lock, stopping shock, tires they squeal and slide!
Cold then hot, what a spot! Freeze then cook then out,
Zip to door, hear the roar! It's time to scream and shout!
Wind blows hair, what a scare! We've never felt such power,
Go faster still, what a thrill! Now sixty miles an hour!
Decelerate, in through gate, glad we buckled tight,
Ride has ended, hands extended, exit ramp in sight!

Hear the roar? Behind the door! New folks taking spins,
We're all through, me with you; walk with drop-jaw grins!
See great displays? Stylin' craze! Brave new world we're in,
Feel the leather, now getting better, hot cars from GM!
Fast cars fun, see them run! But all must do their part,
Lesson there, seat belts wear, with speed be safe and smart!
It's bright outside, see more rides! Across the park we run,
We found more! Let's go Soar! But Test Track was so fun!

Have you ever dreamed that you were flying through the air, free as a bird? In your dream, did your mind soar up, up and away, wheel around, then drop out of the sky at breakneck speed, and then swoop up, up into the blue? As your mind continued in its free spirit dream, did it cruise along at treetop level, across majestic countryside, sail along pounding surf at ocean side, then effortlessly navigate through city skyscrapers at night with their sparking lights? Wow! Sounds like my dream last night!

Disney has captured the above dream in Soarin', a wonderful new ride at EPCOT. How do those Disney Imagineers do it?

Soarin'!

Stroll hand in hand, to EPCOT Land, it's deep in Disney's fair,
The crowd's a-growin' but let's go Soarin'! The line starts over there!
Great Disney fun, the kids all run, a-round then down the hall,
Anticipatin', the Soarin's waitin', a magic ride for all!

Just watch small screen, a flight check scene, it gets us ready to leave,
Scene weaves a spell, but we can tell, it's Disney make-believe!
We're now ready, walk slow and steady, out to Soarin' machine,
Just buckle in, put bags in bin, in front see I-Max screen!

Machine abrupt, it takes us up, sky-high we quickly glide,
The I-Max fades, now river glades, fly down and 'round the side!
The boat folks duck as we soar up, just skimmin' 'long the stream,
Oh wow! And how! Great holy cow! We're spinnin' through a dream!

Fly up now over, the stream ride's over! Now soar through country fair,
From side to side, o'er treetops glide, see skiers over there!
We now hang-glide, oh what a ride! Then golf ball sails right by,
Its Mickey's ball and Fore's the call! Laughing, on we fly!

The scene does change, a mountain range, from country out to sea,
Fly down and 'round, hear ocean sound, whales and dolphins flee!
See surfers tumble, roar and rumble! Waves hit rocks and beach,
Soar breathless rate, see Golden Gate? It's just beyond our reach!

Fly up the bay, we can't delay, and jets go roarin' by,
See super raptor, what's he after? Up in blue-black sky!
Night city scene, our dream machine, flies to Walt's old park,
Bright fireworks flare, oh what a scare! Soarin' in the dark!

Start slowin' down and then to ground, magic ride has ended,
Just hold my hand, can hardly stand! My mind has truly bended!
But now we're ready, holdin' steady, a-walkin' out the doors,
We had such fun, oh what a run! Bold Disney magic Soars!

Are you ready to soar to Mars? The Imagineers at EPCOT make it seem real! Mission: Space is a space flight simulation ride. Guests enter NASA's Mission: Space training center, where they are introduced to the NASA deep space exploration program. They are then divided into groups for introductory space flight training. After flight orientation (and numerous warnings about motion sickness), Guests are strapped into a space capsule for a simulated flight, where of course, the unexpected happens!

Each capsule accommodates a crew of four: commander, pilot, navigator and flight engineer, with a Guest functioning in each role. In contrast to the pre and post-flight hype, the crew's skill and finesse (or lack thereof) in handling their respective roles has nothing to do with the (safe) outcome of the simulated flight.

En route to the main event, Guests pass space hardware, astronaut tributes and memorials, and a cutaway of a huge space station, showing a crew working and living in space. Of course, there is an opportunity to buy souvenirs; after all, this is Disney World! So don your space coveralls, Disneynauts! Grab an air sick bag, and get ready for a trip to Mars!

Disneynauts

Space frontier, mission clear, Mars our goal today!
Pass the gates, spaceship waits, Disneynauts we play!
Choice of ride, must decide, how strong our tummies be,
Rough or smooth, carefully choose, past lunch don't want to see!

Great displays, hopes we raise, our mission will succeed,
Take our places, anxious faces, so many screens to read!
Rumble, roar! To space we soar! Earth now far behind,
Weightless feel, seems so real! Mars I hope we find!

Then to sleep, not a peep, to Mars we coast along,
Up we wake! Goodness sake! In Mars orbit now belong!
Our task to land, Martian sand, descend through fire to ice,
Look and see! Emergency! Will landing skills suffice?

Must be quick! Take the stick! Down and 'round we go,
Runway's short! Can't abort! Hit air brakes much too slow!
It's pucker time! Cut too fine! Pitch and yaw and shift,
Slip and slide, what a ride! Runway ends on cliff!

Finally stop! Edge of drop! Whew! No time to think,
Breathe a sigh; here we lie, teetering on the brink!
Mission over! See Martian rover? Imagine such a ride,
Pale Martian sky, low hills nearby, what's on the other side?

Someday we'll find, what's behind, those hills and dales of Mars!
For now we wait, walk through gate, with dreams of space and stars!
Brave new frontier, our mission clear, on Mars we'll land and stay,
Further still, with time and will, go out to stars someday!

Rain happens, even at Disney World. Some days the skies open up. A deluge inundates every park. Folks scurry for cover after the first few drops; thunder rolls, and shop attendants brace for an onslaught of browsers whose primary objective is to get out of the rain!

Ponchos and umbrellas are the big sellers. Even so, other merchandise attracts the discerning eye, and sometimes, mind you, magic spells occur! I remember such a spell at the EPCOT Mouse Gear Store!

Sorcerer's Hat

My EPCOT stay, a rainy day, sought shelter in a shop,
Past silver fountain still a-spoutin', do raindrops never stop?
Mouse Gear Store, quick in the door! Thunder rolled around,
Adjusted sight to indoor light, and folded umbrella down!
In the gloom across the room, my blinking eyes perceived,
Mickey Mouse! This was his house! He smiled and winked at me!

Noise abated, M. Mouse waited; his spell flowed 'cross the room,
He said: "Just take a look, to shelf in nook, see pale light in gloom?"
A Sorcerer's hat! There it sat! It gave out a pale golden glow,
Spell or dream, gold light streamed! Hat sees! It hears! It knows!
The hat called! It drew me in! I glided slow across the room,
Holy cow! What happens now? Was this a call of doom?

My hands extended, the spell had landed, the hat I must put on,
Couldn't resist it, M. Mouse insisted! Spell was deep and strong!
The Sorcerer's hat! A magic hat! Lights spun high and low,
I put it on! I felt its song! Bright sparkles ebbed and flowed!
World did fade! Mouse magic made! Thunder rolled outside,
Time did stop, no tick or tock, mind whirled high and wide!

But then a sound, a simple sound, a voice in swirling air,
Soft yet firm, the world returned; it said: "Can I help you, sir?"
Bright lights did dim, a store I'm in, I turned and then perceived,
A nice young girl with golden curls, she looked and smiled at me!
"You like the hat, the Sorcerer's hat? Twenty plus tax and fee!"
In a hesitant way, I then did say: "Why yes, I'll take it please!"

She bagged the sale; I paid the bill; then looked through door outside,
Rain had stopped; people hopped, puddles 'tween stores and rides!
Back in the store, just once more, I looked and my eyes perceived,
Mickey the Mouse, safe in his house, he smiled and winked at me!
I left the store, there was so much more, to see and hear and do,
I clutched my bag, with hat inside; I wore it later in my room!

(P.S. I still have my hat!)

Walk through Cinderella's castle in the Kingdom, turn left oblique, and soon you will march into Liberty Square! This lovely enclave replicates a small slice of Revolutionary War America. It includes a beautiful live oak Liberty Tree, the Liberty Square Riverboat, and the Liberty Tree Tavern Restaurant. Popcorn and ice cream stands line the water's edge. Tom Sawyer's Island sits in the small lake just past the riverboat; it's a great place for over-active youngsters to let off a little steam!

In addition to all the above, there are seagulls! These pesky scavengers have complete air supremacy in the skies over the square. They zoom and dive, squawk and screech, and scare you out of your wits when they swoop up from behind and lay a compact wad of poo on top of your head! In a park where Disney controls almost everything (even the mosquitoes aren't allowed to bite), the seagulls are totally out of control! Watch out!

Seagulls!

On Liberty Square, look and beware! Seagulls have stolen the scene,
Hang on to your hat! Watch out for a splat! Swoopin' an' poopin' supreme!
Hear squawkin' an' croakin' on air they're a-floatin', masters of Florida skies,
High wheelin' an' dealin' goodies a-stealin' so hide your hot dogs an' fries!
Unguarded goodies like ice cream and cookies, instant prime targets they be,
So look all around, no food hits the ground; seagulls have radar you see!

Skimmin' an' scammin' even try rammin'; diving from twelve o'clock high,
They'll zoom to your six, a favorite trick; then mess up your hair on the fly!
So what can we do? Just dodge the poo! Ignore their squawkin' an' din,
A-shruggin' and sighin' there's no use denyin'; seagulls always will win!
Just statin' the facts; hide all your snacks! Marauders are waitin' for you,
Struttin' on benches, perched on the fences, ubiquitous pranksters with poo!

Disney cast waits, resigned to their fates, how they stand it don't ask,
They wash the fences; wipe off the benches; clean-up their daily task!
No use to complain, nothing to gain, we're all in the same pooie boat,
Like original sin, seagulls will win, thank goodness for washable coats!
So hide food in a bag and wave the white flag, that's the only recourse,
Even Mickey the Mouse hides in his house when seagulls gather in force!

Numerous times each day, Disney's magic fountain in EPCOT comes alive with pulsing, silver plumes of water and synchronized music. What a show! Each performance lasts about five minutes. The music changes throughout the day and with the seasons. The display mesmerizes everyone around the Innoventions Plaza, even the kids stand quiet!

Look closely! Let your mind roam free! Do ghosts reside within the soaring spray? Each of us will see what we want to see!

Magic Fountain

See Disney magic fountain, sweet sound with water flies,
Bold music set to water jet, grand patterns fill the skies!
Flow higher forever higher, the soaring sparkling spray,
Water prancing, swirling, dancing, timed to music play!
See pirouettes from pulsing jets, each their rhythm send,
Water driven up to heaven, where mist and breezes blend!
See sparkling silver water; hear musical theme upbeat,
Bold bright magic fountain, it cools the summer heat!

A symmetric lovely fountain, in aqua blues and green,
Cataphony and symphony, it creates a shimmering scene!
Misty light adds sheer delight, the music hums with power,
Hold my hand; its wonderland! See rainbows arc the shower!
Bold fantasy blends to whimsy, the jets they pulse all around,
Spraying water ever higher, silver circles timed with sound!
Misty showers now overpowers, see figures at edge of sight,
Fountain magic fountain, pale ghosts meet bright sunlight!

Surreal yet real this fountain, ghosts dance in silver spray,
They meet and seek the plaza, for us to watch them play!
Look to see and true believe; bold spray leaps high to show,
Just peer within! Let dance begin! A ballet in misty glow!
Ghosts we find swirl to rhyme; they spin and leap so gay,
I've now lost track, the water slack, the music dies away!
Was it real or just surreal? Did patterns touch the skies?
Was Disney's fountain magic; should we trust our eyes?

Now leave bright silver fountain, our awe has passed to bliss,
Heard music play saw water spray; saw ghosts in silver mist!
It's time to walk 'round EPCOT town, but we'll come back to see,
Silver water prancing, swirling, dancing; so bold and fancy free!
Look for pirouettes from pulsing jets, to each their rhythm send,
See water driven high to heaven, where mist and breezes blend!
We'll again watch soaring water; with bold music theme upbeat,
It will spout from magic fountain, and cool the summer heat!

Please stand clear of the doors! (Now repeat in Spanish!) Every visitor to Disney World remembers the monorail!

There are three monorail lines at Disney World, with nearly fourteen miles of elevated track. Two lines circle the Seven Seas Lagoon. The "express" carries day guests to the Magic Kingdom from the Ticket and Transportation Center (TTC). The local, for Disney resort guests, makes stops at the TTC and all three resorts around the lagoon: the Polynesian, the Grand Floridian, and the Contemporary. The third line runs from the TTC to EPCOT.

The EPCOT line is longest and most scenic; however, my favorite is still the local ride to the Magic Kingdom. Somehow, going to the Kingdom seems the most "Disney." Also, it's fun to watch families on the way. The following poem may bring back memories!

Monorail!

See the train; it comes 'round again; we'll ride the skyway trail,
Inward bound; hear swishing sound, our sleek smooth monorail!
The conductor smiles; go past turnstiles; then slide across the seat,
Make room for more; close the door! Escape from summer heat!
Make smooth transition; its air conditioned; glide along the way,
Around the lake, for goodness sake! Magic Kingdom for today!

Past the Grand, hold my hand; the ride seems fresh and new,
Past magic door, we'll then explore, just past the perfect view!
Train arches high; we touch the sky; our ride's so silky smooth,
Sleek monorail to our fairy tale, it's time to re-live our youth!
So hard to wait, but we anticipate, the train provides the way,
We're just like kids, dare not miss, our Magic Kingdom day!

The kids have ants in their pants, they squirm and push and pull,
Some in strollers, some on shoulders, Dads with backpacks full!
Mommy look! It's like my storybook! See high castle over there?
It's our station! Mickey's waitin'! Got chewing gum in my hair!
Poor Mom all frazzled, kids all dazzled, they fidget and they fuss,
Old folks smile, it's been awhile, since small kids belonged to us!

Now our train, slows down again, on Disney's high skyway trail,
The Kingdom found, oh happy sound! Kids leave the monorail!
They're down the ramp, skippitty scamp; just let them run ahead,
Us old folks walk and just quiet talk, now can hear what's said!
Just anticipate and walk slow to gate; a pleasant start this day,
Hear background, a swishing sound, our train just glides away!

Disney cruises deliver all of what most folks love about Disney World: beautiful themed accommodations and innovative dining, romantic evenings and unique family style entertainment. On board ships Disney Wonder and Disney Magic, there's even more: pampering spa treatments, three swimming pools (one for kids, one for families, and one for adults only), and for sports enthusiasts, a lounge with screens that present sporting events from all over the world. Theatrical entertainment includes full-scale stage productions that feature Disney songs, story lines, and beautifully detailed sets. The two theaters on board each ship are so plush that it's easy to snuggle in and doze while waiting for the show to start! (I'm very good at this.)

The ships cruise at sea, visit Nassau and other Caribbean ports, and dock for a day at Castaway Cay, Disney's private island in the Bahamas. Shopping, beaches, water sports, and romantic private places: Disney provides it all! Hey Linda, are you ready to go cruisin' again?

Wonder!

On Disney ship Wonder, just you with me; we'll leave home port, rove the blue seas,
We'll sail this evening, taking our ease; watching the seabirds, enjoying the breeze!
A bold classic liner, with subtle soft themes, Mickey's here; he winks and he beams,
We'll stand by the rail; a gold sunset gleams; Nassau bound, on a ship of dreams!
Enjoy gourmet dinner, so blissful the hour; then stroll on top deck; see evening star,
After go dancing, champagne at the bar, white wake streaming, see lights from afar!
On stateroom veranda, we'll sit at our ease; stars will come out; hold hands with me,
Then later to bed, you'll smile at me; my old eyes will twinkle; we'll share love at sea!
We're cruising with Wonder; just you with me, in our little world, sail the broad seas,
Romance is so simple; we're easy to please; a couple of lovebirds, enjoying the breeze!

Next day the gold dawn, sleepy our smiles, coffee will perk; get dressed in high style,
After breakfast, down gangway we'll file; shop for trinkets, on Nassau's gold mile!
Late we'll return, with small treasures from land; spa is a-waiting, isn't love grand?
Massage for couples, supple soft hands, oils and sweet fragrance, relax and pretend!
Our ship will then sail, off to Castaway Cay; we'll be there by morning, over the seas,
But our dinner's at eight, Palos will please; romantic fine dining, sunset and breeze!
Visit Cadillac Lounge, hear piano soft play; hear musical memories, end to our day,
We're still young at heart, though hair has turned gray; you with me, what can I say?
We'll cruise with Wonder, roving the seas, our own little world, so eager to please!
Romance is so simple, just take our ease, a couple of old birds, enjoying the seas!

Dock Castaway Cay; will you walk with me? Leave our fine ship; view azure blue seas?
Beach and palm trees, we'll be at ease, then soar with the seabirds, high on the breeze!
Old pirate ship waits; it sets fantasy theme; of course it's pretend, but we can dream,
We'll walk the soft sand; like snow it will gleam; pick up sea shells; feel the sun beam!
Find lemonade stand, so blissful our tour; then stroll along surf, slow waves re-assure,
Stroll adults only beach, mid-morning the hour, time to ourselves, touch water so pure!
Then a barbeque lunch, soft drinks from the bar, sit in the shade; pass the noon hour,
Small boat to the reef, get sea-spray shower; thundering surf, feel nature's raw power!
Look to the Wonder, safe as you please, like a scene on a postcard, in from the seas,
Our romance is so simple; just take our ease, a couple of seabirds, feel the salt breeze!

Our last day will dawn; we sailors become, tanned and fit, broad seas we did roam,
Whitecaps around us, bow wave with sea foam, dolphins to guide us, sailing for home!
The Wonder sails smoothly, no pitches nor roll; eat and be merry, our epicurean goal,
Like pale golden wine, we age soft and slow, now time to enjoy, life's evening glow!
On stateroom veranda, we'll relax as we please; shady and cool, feel the brisk breeze,
You'll hold my hand, soft kiss give to me, my eyes will twinkle, know love that will be!
One last dance, in our private way, then we'll stand by the rail and view the night sky,
We're still young at heart, though hair has turned gray; you with me, what can I say?
We'll cruise with Wonder; rove the broad seas, our own little world, so easy to please!
Romance is so simple, just take our ease, a couple of lovebirds, enjoying the breeze!

Disney loves a parade! Each theme park has its own set, and they constantly evolve. Every one of the "parades" is special and unique, and there are always crowds!

The Magic Kingdom currently has three (2009): the Wishes Nighttime Spectacular, Celebrate a Dream Come True and the current version of Spectro-Magic. Of course, every evening also includes fireworks and Tinker Bell at Cinderella's Castle. An evening parade followed later by fireworks is a wonderful way to end a day at the Magic Kingdom. Spectators line the curb and sidewalks long before each event. I've often wished that I stood eight feet tall so I could see!

EPCOT has Illuminations and Reflections of Earth, which sometimes has an associated parade. EPCOT had an especially elaborate parade during the millennia celebration in the year 2000. If you have big bucks, boats can be chartered and the Illuminations display can be viewed from a boat on the World Showcase Lagoon. What a show!

Disney's Hollywood Studios currently has the Block Party Bash (2009). In the past, the Studios did a lot with the Toy Story theme and variations on motor cars and movie stars. The long running Fantasmic is more of a fireworks and laser show than a parade, but it does have parade elements, including a water pageant with canoes and a showboat!

The Animal Kingdom has Mickey's Jammin' Jungle Parade, which has a variation called Mickey's Jingle Jungle Parade during the Christmas Holidays. The stilt walkers are especially colorful and delightful!

There is also the long running Electrical Water Pageant, which is a "parade" of barges around the Seven Seas Lagoon and Bay Lake. Magic Kingdom Resort guests are treated to this charming display almost every evening!

The following verses celebrate just four of the Disney "parades." I could go on forever, but four stanzas give you a good sample. Enjoy!

Parade!

Oh, what a magical evening; oh, what a wonderful day,
Everything's lovely this evening; think I'll watch a parade!
A special evening for wishes; your dreams may all come true,
A parade strolls down Main Street; Mickey's a-coming in view!
He waves to crowds on the sidewalk; he smiles to me and to you,
Bright floats all pass at curbside; with lights in every bold hue!
Oh, what a picturesque ending; we've had a wonderful day,
A spectra-magical evening; a-watching the Main Street parade!

Oh, what a fantasmic evening; oh, what a spectacular day,
A story to tell this evening; we can sit and watch the display!
Mickey's dream goes a-wishing; stars all dance to his tune,
The comets and lasers go swishing; fireworks fly to the moon!
The canoes and showboat a-coming; around and into full view,
Characters wave to the grandstand, spectacular pass in review!
Oh, what a perfect ending; we've seen Mickey's magic display,
Fantasmic world this evening; now stardust sprinkles our way!

Oh, what an animal-like evening; let's watch a safari at play,
The jungle's a-jamming this evening; think I'll watch the parade!
Mickey's a-leading the animals; they wiggle and waddle in view,
With lions and leopards all leaping; the birds in every bright hue!
Stilt walkers a-dancing and prancing; how they do it don't know,
They go in and 'round then up and down; what a colorful show!
Oh, what a roaring great evening; an enchanting end to our day,
A-jimmin' and jammin' in jungle; a wild and exciting parade!

Oh, what a silky soft evening; oh, what a perfect array,
The torch lights glow this evening, think I'll watch the display!
Buildings sparkle with white lights; the lake glows golden so bright,
Then stop! It's a moment of quiet; the torches dim to dark night!
Reflections of Earth in the starlight; then lasers shoot for the moon,
Then flashes and crashes of fireworks; the Earth turns slow to a tune!
We then have a glorious finale; the lasers all flash and display,
Illuminations done for this evening; reflections on ending our day!

Fairy tales and castles have long been part of the Disney experience. Cinderella's Castle touches something deep within our souls; we want to believe in love and happy endings!

Every time I walk by the castle in the Magic Kingdom, I secretly look up to one of the high windows. In my mind, I see a beautiful Princess, just back in the shadows! I think of the Disney song, and I know that someday, her Prince will come. Like the Princess, I often walk within a wonderful fairy tale, and I believe in happy endings!

Castle

Castle, castle, soaring high, slender spires that touch the sky,
I wonder if, I wonder why, a Princess dwells in tower so high!
Does she hope, does she wait, for love to come from far away?
A voice so soft, from window sigh, clear and sweet, on breezes fly,
In twilight gleam, hope and dream, lovers bound, blissful scene!
Hear her song; it soft does flow, on quiet evening, in golden glow!
Angels smile, the future see, a dream fulfilled, her love will be!
I wish it so, it must be so; her song forlorn, on breeze does flow!

Castle, castle, turrets round, see high window, hear sweet soft sound,
Wonder if her Prince can hear, her song of love with words so clear?
Will her words reach his ear, and will he come and hold her near?
Does he dream a dream like mine, and will he seek true love divine?
Does he perceive a special way to join with her, though far away?
From distant scene, I know he sees, castle high, he wants to please,
I see him smile, he knows, he sees, dream fulfilled, their love will be!
His heart knows, it must be so, he hears love's song in evening glow!

Castle, castle, dream or real, your shapely stones know how I feel,
I wonder if, I wonder how, will all our dreams fulfill somehow?
Prince and Princess, me with you, hand in hand, to dream and do,
Believe within; true love will win, on this we hope, new lives begin!
Like Prince and Princess, shall we share, kisses soft with sweet caress?
Now here I stand, impatient wait; but soon we'll meet, near castle gate,
Angels smile, though I may dream, we'll then share love's bliss serene!
I believe it so, it must be so; I hear love's song, the breeze does know!

As a final note in this chapter, many frequent visitors to Disney World have acquired a new hobby. Look for hidden Mickeys!

Hidden Mickeys

Mickey the Mouse has a humorous way,
Of peeking 'round corners and watching you play!
On walls, in halls and high on trapezes
In treeses on keyses, wherever he pleases!

The houses have mouses and so do the rides,
On stools, in pools and turnstile guides!
In roses, on clotheses, with Donald the Duck,
On hats and bats and huge coffee cups!

High in the sky on clouds so poofy,
See Mickey with Minnie laughing at Goofy!
Hidden unbidden on Dumbo's left ear,
Ubiquitous Mickeys, new ones each year!

Imagineers smile, they have sly fun,
Hiding new Mickeys in Florida sun!
Just look in the book if you need a clue,
Tricky old Mickey is waiting for you!

4. REFLECTIONS

Some of the poems in this chapter hold up a mirror. In this mirror, we see aspects of ourselves and of our world. Others show a path that we may choose to follow. If we choose wisely, the path will lead to fulfillment. Most of these "reflection" poems are happy; a few are sad. Many have a softly "spiritual" point of view; yet they do not espouse any particular religion. Others muse quietly on the trials of life and a few are quite poignant. Others present ghostly visions! Some tell stories about ways of life and happy times that are gone forever, and a few are cynical in a funny sort of way.

There is no particular grouping of the poems by category in this chapter; they tend to follow the order in which they were written. Thus, the reader may skip around with no loss of continuity. In any case, read and enjoy, beginning with an old fashioned country good morning!

Country folk get out of bed early. In the old days, before moving to town, we milked the cows, fed the chickens, and so on. Even now, after years in town, we tend to follow old habits. The cows and chickens live only in our memories, but we still like the pale dawn, birds that are newly awake, and the crisp, cool air. For me, Angels peek through the morning mist between earth and sky. It is a good time to think, to reflect, and to prepare. Good morning! It's the best time of day!

Morning!

Sun in the morning peeps over the rise,
Breeze touches trees, gold lights the skies!
Souls strive for heaven, birds take to wing,
Angels have homes here, softly they sing!

Happy this morning, forget the dark night,
Light brings new meaning, to each soul's delight!
Bird song says: "Welcome! Hello my good friends!"
Sweet sound the song here, to heaven it wends!

Peace in the morning gold light all around,
Shadows now faded, good memories abound!
Bring candle for accent, no cares for awhile,
Window belongs here, greet dawn with a smile!

So still this morning, now step out the door,
Breathe the clean air, touch morning warm glow!
Now walk to the garden, greet blossoms so new,
Colors all 'round here, flowers glisten with dew!

Glory this morning our sun rises slow,
Light beams inspire us, eyes twinkle and glow!
Dreams we shall follow, to path we will run,
Contentment we find here, new day has begun!

Mothers sing to children. I remember this song from my childhood. My Mother sang it softly, to a tune as old as the hills. I'll give you the words; you can imagine the tune.

Our Dream

When nighttime comes I'll sleep my best,
Of you I'll dream, I'll be at rest.

Though I sleep, I true believe,
As I dream, you dream with me.

Our dream comes, our souls do go,
To magic land, in sunshine glow.

They'll takes us in, and bless our day,
Sing songs sweetly, a familiar way.

Though we sleep, I true believe,
As we dream, we live and breathe.

When you awake, and start your day,
Hold our dream, come what may.

Night will come; we'll join again,
Our shared dream, that never ends!

Sometimes the cold wind howls outside the door, and sinister spirits rule the night! It is good to stay inside, near the fire, and hope for a better morning!

Winter's Eve

Winter's eve with wind and snow, sit by fire, lights down low!
You and I, cozy and warm, we'll stay inside, safe from harm.

Wind brings voices, tales of woe, world of cares outside our door!
Morning light we'll face the day, meet the challenge come what may.

This eve we'll sit, by calm firelight, take my hand, fear not the night!
Read my eyes, look deep inside, find my soul, where love resides.

Look through window, world at bay, this night is ours, inside we'll stay!
You and I, cozy and warm, fire burns bright, we're safe from harm.

Sooner or later, we all loose someone we love. Try as we might in our minds, we cannot bring them back. It is a terrible feeling. Adults also have the responsibility to explain death to young children, even as we deal with our own hearts.

Line of Stones

I close my eyes, I seek the night; a vision comes, in pale moonlight.
My mind sees, just down the road, a line of stones, stark and bold.

Graven names, dates and places, reminds us all, lost smiles and faces.
Her body sleeps; her soul has flown; I must face life; I'm so alone!

I see her face; she smiles at me; I reach out; her hand I seek.
She turns and walks in soft pale mist, and disappears, in heaven's bliss.

Clock ticks loud, from lonely room, marking time, the sound of doom.
Words can't tell, how it feels, to live with loss that time can't heal!

Taylor: I think about Grandma a lot. I know you do too!-Grandpa.

Grandma (For Taylor)

'Round every corner, just out of sight,
Grandma is smiling, heaven's delight!
She's always there, but you cannot see,
Her love surrounds both you and me!

You miss her deeply, but know in your heart,
She feels your sorrow, to live now apart.
She wants you happy, not sad all the time,
Live to the fullest, love and be kind!

Ryan: Grandma is special. We both miss her a lot. Listen to what your heart tells you! –Grandpa

---

Grandma (For Ryan)

When you sit quiet, think softly of me,
I watch over you, though you cannot see.
Do all your best, follow your star,
I'll follow your progress, wherever you are!

Know that I'm happy, heaven's delight,
Flowers every day, stars twinkle each night.
You miss me true, but know in your heart,
You too should be happy, though we're apart!

Judy: Linda understands my feelings. She soothes my troubled soul. We walk our golden path. Until we meet again, smile and be at peace. Love, Frank.

Death Do Us Part

We lived and loved warm in the sun; now for you, life's joy is done.
You've passed to heaven and I remain; here on earth but not the same!

My years do pass; life goes on; I often dream and hear your song.
Now you walk midst heaven's flowers; your time stands still; there are no hours!

We share thoughts; I see your face; you smile and move with youth and grace.
You've shed your years in heaven's glow; I'm now old, on earth below!

September's here; I've found new love; I know you see and smile above.
You too have found in heaven's bliss; friends anew and love's warm kiss!

You are happy; friends hold your hand; I smile for you; through tears I'm glad.
I miss you dear; it can't be changed, the fate we have, it's been ordained!

Some days I'm sad on memory lane; but mostly glad, I slowly mend.
New promise made until life's end; I'll stay on earth; love blooms again!

We'll move on, when our lives end; we'll meet with you and touch your hand.
Time will stop, there'll be no hours; contented souls midst heaven's flowers!

The Christmas season brings joy, gifts, and love. Preparations for the present holiday include shopping, Christmas cards, and setting up holiday decorations. Some are new, but many are extracted from dusty boxes that have multiplied over the years. Old decorations bring back memories of Christmases past. Often the memories are accompanied with tears. I try to smile and dwell on the good times; but there are difficult days.

Judy, it has been almost three years since you passed to heaven. I know you are in a better place, but I miss you so. Please have a Happy Christmas!

Linda, you comfort me on sad days, I do not know what I would do without you.

Thanks for understanding!

Old Christmas Lights

Christmas lights like memories, bright happy times recall,
In boxes lay all put away and stacked against the wall!
Third Christmas now but yet somehow it seems but yesterday,
We shopped a lot and bought those lights in dusty boxes lay!
It's been so long; we had our song; yet in my heart I know,
Can't stay sad, new memories add, to ours in silver glow!
I've found new love, you approve, so Christmas time this year,
We'll add a light on Christmas night, and smile for you my dear!

In Christmas show old memories flow; eyes turn misty gray,
She holds my hand, shares her love; makes sadness fade away!
I know I am a lucky man, for I've found new love my dear,
It's not the end; I start again! New love I share this year!
This year I'll shop until I drop, with loving wife in tow,
Peace we'll find, ties that bind, in Christmas golden glow!
She walks with me; I know you see, from heaven high above,
We'll add a light for your delight and smile for you with love!

Walked today to your grave, so many stories there,
Your place among so many, soft voices on the air!
Christmas wreaths and holly leaves decorate some stones,
For you I found a silver crown; I stood there not alone!
A windy day and some who say, the snow will come on down,
A blanket white for your delight, ice crystals for your crown!
A Christmas light in the night will shine from high above,
It does show for those who know that heaven sends us love!

This Christmas night will bring insight and happy times recall,
We'll pause awhile, I know you smile, and bless our love and all!
Third Christmas now, yet somehow, it seems just yesterday,
We laughed and touched, loved so much, hearts were young and gay!
It's been so long since our song, yet in my heart I know,
You smile and say it's time to play and share the golden glow!
So we'll sigh and then apply the lessons of our years,
We'll add a light for your delight and smile for you my dear!

With love for two wonderful ladies, past and present, from Frank.

Have you ever awakened at night in a cold sweat and glimpsed a shadow outside the window? Was it a dream or something more? Sometimes ghosts rule the night!

The Man Who Wasn't There

I saw him standing in the night, by the window, pale moonlight;
Near a tree with limbs so bare, a tall gray man who wasn't there!

A hooded head, no face to see, a white cold mist about his feet.
Yet he observed, a sightless stare, this bold cold man who wasn't there!

In my bed I sat up straight, my pillow soaked in clammy sweat.
I shivered cold, he didn't care, this ghostly man who wasn't there!

He raised a hand, he pointed slow, through the window, moonlight glow.
"Soon!" said he, "you'll see my lair," this beckoning man who wasn't there!

"Darkness waits, it is your fate, you'll join me; your hour is late;
Your soul is mine 'til judgment fair, at heaven's gate, I'll take you there!"

"With me you'll rest until that day, your lifeless body will decay!"
"You'll follow me, but don't despair," said the man who wasn't there!

"Why fear Death?' His voice was soft, "At heaven's gate you will again,
Meet your friends and memories share," cajoled the man who wasn't there!

"Wait!" I cried. "What must I do?" I'm not set to go with you!"
"I must right my lifelong cares; have pity man, you were not there!"

"When I chose my life to spend, I didn't plan that it must end!
Where were you to guide my fare?" I asked the man who wasn't there!

"I know now that I've grown old, but give me time to right my soul!"
"I will go when I have shared," I bargained as he waited there!

Then he said: "If you've lived a worthy life, you'll re-unite with loving wife!"
She passed this way, she's in my care," a whispered voice caressed my ear!

"It's not so bad, for you may see, at heaven's gate your family!"
"But of course, you must have shared, fruits of life, with those who cared!"

I cried aloud: "What must I do; before I spend my time with you?"
"On judgment day, what is my fate? Will I walk through that golden gate?"

"Will the gate be shut; that is my fear; what must I do, with Death so near?"
"Comfort me, my faith renew, give me guidance; what must I do?"

Silence weighed upon my soul; Death stood still, and time passed slow.
Then words came, so stark yet fair, from the man who wasn't there!

"The good Lord knows grief you bear; seek his grace, he waits; he cares!"
"Future brings new love and dreams; life goes on, though hard it seems!"

"You must adapt and end your strife; in time allowed, fulfill your life!"
"With open heart you'll find a way; seek happy times, rejoice each day!"

"World turns 'round; walk your path; find life's wisdom; fear not Death!"
"Give of yourself; seek truth each night; the future's here; follow the light!"

"I'll come one day! Yet while light gleams, use your time, and follow dreams!"
"Hear my message! Yet do not fear; my image fades, for I'm not here!"

I lay back and closed my eyes, I pondered life, heard dawn breeze sigh.
Death will come, and this I know, he will point, and I will go!

Yet past the grave white light gleams; I will fulfill and live my dreams!
I've found love, new wife who shares, a golden path far down the years!

My first love, now in the grave, wishes joy to those who live!
I have faith and true believe, she warmly smiles and knows I grieve.

For two now love me; I'm truly blessed, a second chance for happiness!
A message given, I no longer fear; the tall gray man who isn't here!

Memories and ghosts dwell at the edges of sight and sound. They especially haunt old familiar places. Sometimes they are nostalgic and welcome; they cause a smile over a remembered moment. Sometimes however, memories and ghosts dampen a new joy and cloud the future in a mist of remembrance, times and events that are gone forever!

Ghosts

Old places, ghost faces, swirl in and around,
Share and despair, they smile and they frown!
They walk while we talk; I see them at night,
Can't shut them out nor send them to flight!

No sleep so deep to make a new dream,
I try, they sigh, eyes twinkle and gleam!
Memories of glories haunt my cold soul,
Need places and faces where ghosts can't go!

Seek peace, dreams cease, find bright rising sun,
Seek light and delight, my life should be fun!
New places and faces, your smile guides the way,
Can't live in sorrow, please ghosts go away!

Years pass quickly; grey hair crowns ours heads; wrinkles appear. We walk slower, sit more often, and muse quietly on long winter evenings. Memories of youth pass before our eyes, slowly. We savor the good times and set aside the bad. We have regrets. My goodness, how time flies!

Friday Evening

Remember our days, out on the town,
We danced and we sang, never a frown?!
Now we stay home, each Friday night,
Sit by the fire, watch shadows and light!

Huddle in close, try to stay warm,
Eyes still twinkle, your hand on my arm!
We fondly remember, days in the sun,
When love was new, hearts became one!

We sowed and we reaped, harvest all gold,
Now we wait, our story winds low.
Glories now over, twilight is here,
Leaves fly by window, winter is near!

Shadows do flicker, wind moans so low,
Pictures and voices, old stories flow!
Some from the past, but others are new,
Firelight shows future, swirls into view.

Savor the moment, starlight above,
Hearts remain young, filled with our love!
We'll face the night, your hand on my arm,
Love you and keep you, safe from night's harm!

Winter evenings foster a melancholy spirit. The first snow of the season swirls in the air and gently falls to ground. Gray skies and early sundown touch on our senses, cold damp air chills our bones and wayward memories weigh on our souls. It is a time to sit by the fire and seek balance within.

First Snow

First snow this year, touch autumn gold, summer ended, story that's told.
Silver streaks in gray cold sky, chill damp air, wind moans, trees sigh.

We've sown and reaped, now we bear, fruits of our days from summer fair.
Some of it bad, but mostly it's good, fruit we've stored winter's grey mood.

Sit by the fire; we think of days past, savor good fruit, put aside bad.
Yet bad is there in small cold dish, must sample its flavor in spite of our wish.

Flavor of moments we prefer to forget, times of grief, words we regret.
First snow this winter, softly it falls, maybe the snow will cover it all.

Take dish of bad fruit, open the door, snow blows in, white on the floor.
Set dish outside, snow blankets all, freezing bad fruit, beyond our recall.

Look out the window, the dish outside, freezes and covers, bad memories hide.
Close door to cold, go sit by warm fire, savor good fruit, smile and be glad.

Soft white blanket covers our minds, forgive and forget, as seekers we find;
Time and first snow, eases the pain, grey turns to night, peace we gain!

Good fruit we've saved golden its glow, slowly we savor, as lover's we know,
Memories of pleasure let winter wind blow, inside we're warm in firelight glow!

Did you ever wonder how and why your life unfolds? Do our lives just follow a script that has already been written? Or can we look at alternatives, see consequences, and then freely choose?

Chest of Drawers

In my mind I look and see,
A chest of drawers in front of me.
Each drawer has dreams and songs to sing,
Which shall I open, and be those things?

When we are born at heaven's gate,
We get a chest that holds our fate.
Open some drawers and some do not,
We make choices and live our lot.

An old drawer open, what do I see,
A pale gold moon, a silver key.
I unlocked my soul and was the dream,
And walked the sand by shining sea.

Now close that drawer, to memory send,
A long lovely dream that had its end.
A new drawer open, what must I do,
To live the dream and walk with you?

Gold key there, and though it's late,
I touch it slow, to learn my fate.
I chose this drawer and seek to find,
Peace and love and ties that bind.

When I close this last you'll see,
Night will come, an evening scene,
From chest of drawers I'll walk away
My world will end, a lovely day!

Time for a change of pace. A bit of whimsy seems appropriate. Mathematicians will tell you that even chaos has patterns. Look closely and you will see!

Patterns

I see patterns in the oddest places,
Clouds in the sky and people's bland faces,
Tidal ebb in crystal clear pools,
Flights of fantasy and the talk of fools!

There are patterns to love and patterns to hate,
Hate is strong with uncertain fate!
I prefer love, a pattern to choose,
But love is soft, so easy to loose!

Rills on water, with dappled light,
Patterns abound, to my soul's delight!
All have rhythm in this game I play,
I view the world in the oddest way!

Find insight in patterns; just use your mind,
Faces and places, patterns we find!
Look for the rhythm, patience the key,
Make some sense from the world we see!

Dreams sometimes allow us to find peace and joy, and we awake refreshed. Let your soul fly high in the night; visions await! Time flows either fast or very slow, it your choice. Sometimes in my dreams I visit the angels!

Angels!

When night arrives, it must be said,
I dream a lot when I'm in bed.
The day is done, greet velvet night,
Now soar my soul, in peaceful flight!

'Tween earth and sky I seek the space
Where I meet angels face to face!
They silver glow in black midnight,
And smile at me with warm delight!

I rise to greet each one on high,
And touch their wings as they fly by!
My soul is free as I dream on,
Harp music drifts in joyous song!

We soar and drift above the earth,
Night dream hope for new day birth!
Cares wisp away, and light shines through,
A path to heaven runs straight and true!

Dream 'til dawn, then back to bed,
Angels smile and slowly fade.
I am content, I saw the path,
To heaven's gate, though dream has passed.

Have you noticed how time flows fast or slow, depending on what you are doing? For example, workdays sometimes drag on forever. On the other hand, weekends just zip on by in the blink of an eye! Let's take the concept of the variable speed of time to an extreme; the only limitations are those of relativity and imagination!

It's About Time!

As Einstein so aptly stated,
Space and time are related!
The faster I go, the slower time flows,
But light shines constant and unabated!

I look across a dizzy space
And stop the time, all things in place!
Expand my mind, new insight sought,
The air is filled with whispered thought!

Survey still faces, for I must know,
What character shows when no time flows!
Look behind the frozen smiles,
Find hidden meanings and unsaid guiles!

Survey all things, let mind walk slow,
Seek small details both high and low!
Look for beauty, find tiny things,
Like sparkling light on angel's wings!

Beyond the people and small details,
A new world waits over hills and dales!
I seek the space 'tween earth and light,
Where shadows play and dreams delight!

Among the shadows, new paths trace,
They lead away in time and space!
I soar on high and look below,
Each path shines for me to know!

I look for signs; they're plain to see,
When time stands still and mind is free!
I soar along and look for clues,
Rank-order paths, then freely choose!

Have you ever walked in woodland just before sunrise and wondered what the new day would bring? I have! Hope for a bright new day may spring up in your heart, just before the golden sunrise. Look to the east just before dawn, through the trees. What do you see through the morning mist?

Shadow Wood

World at rest before new dawn,
Dew drops patter on dead leaf ground.
Pale east sky accents the gloom
In shadow wood 'neath cold white moon!

Mist creeps slow through silent trees,
Soft wisps rise from last year's leaves.
Night is over, but new day waits,
A silent moment, to ponder fate.

What will I see when shadows raise,
Sun-lit green or soft white haze?
Choice needs light, fog hides the scene,
I seek a path, from cold night's dream!

Cool morn breeze now stirs my soul,
Let dawn's new light touch leaf and bough!
Wisp mist away, no fog pale white,
See gold on green, leaves shining bright!

Pale blue sky, the sun peeps through,
I see my path, runs straight and true!
A rising sun, the night now past,
Shadows fade, new day at last!

Heaven's promise, tree tops green,
Take path through woods, fulfill the dream!
Gold dappled leaves, a bright sun morn,
Shadows flee, new hope is born!

Review the dream, check signs on path,
Match signs to dream, time flies fast!
Conscience guides, walk straight and true,
Future smiles when sun shines through!

Time to change the mood again, this time with a poem about a way of life that few even remember! It may therefore come as a surprise to modern readers, but the fur trade still exists! A few trappers still apply their ancient skills; they mostly work in Canada, Alaska and northern Minnesota. A few, a very few, still trap the rivers and streams in the rural Midwest.

In my youth, over fifty years ago, I knew many trappers and fur buyers. They were mostly older men; I was one of the few youngsters in the game. They were a colorful lot. One was a Spanish-American War veteran; he charged up San Juan Hill with Teddy Roosevelt, or so he said. Another was a hard-drinking old pirate; he had a wooden leg! There were several World War veterans. Old Ogle McGrew was a former Seabee who fought in the South Pacific during World War II. Before that, he served in the Merchant Marine in the North Atlantic during World War I! Old Ogle taught me how to tell whether or not a muskrat hole was currently occupied. He laughed a lot, mostly at me!

Finally, there was my father. He trapped the Wabash River valley for over thirty years. He was the best shot with a rifle that I have ever known. He could trap mink, muskrats, raccoons, and a dozen other critters with amazing skill and consistency. He could see well in the dark, walk a dozen miles each day, every day, and still have time to teach and love his only son, me! He died at age eighty-seven. I miss him.

Those "old men" taught me many things. The most important were: a love for the outdoors, a deep respect for the natural world, and an appreciation for all life. I learned to love the creatures that I trapped; their lives were taken with the knowledge that all life is precious. Nothing was wasted.

I miss those days. However, there is a time to hunt, a time to play, and a time to sit and recall the day!

Trapper's Rest

Silent shadow, sure and slow, a trapper's lonely way,
Wade in stream, pale light gleam, before cold dawn each day!
Winter fair, feel clean air, ice trims the streambed edge,
Water tinkles, makes silver ripples, there's snow on limestone ledge!
Hear rustling sounds, dark surrounds, eyes from shadows glow,
Small creatures creep, shelters seek, in bushes dense and low!
Set steel traps among the gaps, in trails for fur-clad game,
So long ago, memories flow, I waded woodland stream!
Learned the lore, high and low, sun and moon and birth,
Life and death, nature's breath, secrets close to earth!

Mink and fox among the rocks, hunt the silver stream,
Lives at bay, seek their prey, the way it's always been!
Beavers build, willows yield; tooth meets wood each day,
Homes and more, food to store, dams the stream delay!
Rabbits ramble, lives they gamble, danger high above,
See hawks in sky, they silent glide, spying every move!
Muskrats gather, raccoons finger, food in cleansing pools,
Feed beds full, crayfish pull, observe; apply the trapper's tools!
Learn the lore, there's always more, sun and moon and birth,
Life and death, nature's breath, secrets from the earth!

Trapper's art, become a part, nature's timeless way,
Feel web of life, birth and death, each a role to play!
See a den, how long it's been, since muskrat entered in?
Touch the sides, if hand smooth slides, muskrats hide within!
Observe the tracks, creatures walk, across the soggy ground,
Learn each print, nature's hint, game that moves around!
November clime, the fur is prime, wade the icy stream,
Set traps and wait, game to take, winter's annual dream!
Apply the lore; there's always more, sun and moon and birth,
Life and death, nature's breath, become a part with earth!

Trap chain to stake, deep water waits, hands turn icy numb,
Trap now set; make a bet, that game this night will come!
Apply the scent, habits meant; attract the game you see,
They follow nose to set enclosed, captured they will be!
Build dirt hole set for foxes; know raccoons come to meat,
But beavers glide to dams at night, trap in spillway greet!
But mink so sly finds muskrat slide a baby kit to steal,
Now trap is set so mink will get, caught instead of meal!
Apply the lore, on streambed shore, sun and moon and birth,
Know life and death, nature's breath, gifts of mother earth!

Home each night, use skinning knife, clean the daily catch,
By dim light, prepare the hides; make the stretchers match!
Hang fur to dry, on line up high, across the tool shed wall,
Store the meat, use to make, new bait for creatures call!
Collect scent glands, store in cans, messy business seems,
But trapper's way, no waste this day, every part redeem!
Clean the knife, late at night, pack for next day's run,
Soon new dawn, must sleep again and rise before the sun!
Apply the lore and wade once more, sun for new day birth,
Life then death, nature's breath, from earth to life to earth!

So long ago, my memories flow; I see the woodland stream,
Sure and slow, my shadows grow; it's but a distant dream!
Half century now, but yet somehow, it seems just yesterday,
Lone trapper's song, hum along, and icy streambed wade!
Pause a while, wistful smile, my youth and wild land's call,
This winter's night I seek insight, a woodland scene recall!
Now sit and sigh, in dreams apply, nature's lore delight,
Traps I set; make the bet, that game will come this night!
Recall the lore, high and low, sun and moon and birth,
Life and death, trapper's rest, return to mother earth!

Every child finds exciting new worlds just outside the door! Read books, expand the mind, and prepare yourself; an exciting world awaits!

Country Kitchen

Long long ago, on county dirt road,
See little farm house, a refuge from cold.
Start of a journey, humble and poor,
It began in the kitchen and led out the door.

Look in the window, shining so bright,
Lamp on the table, dancing gold light.
Shadows at bay in corners of room,
Grandma at stove, father home soon.

Boy at the table, reading a book,
Imagines new worlds, can tell by his look.
He peers out the window, stares at night sky,
Eyes unseeing, but his mind soars high!

It began with a book, read with delight,
His world expanded, beyond kitchen light!
Grandma smiles, she knows and sees,
Boy will grow tall and follow his dreams.

What book did he read, to unlock his mind?
What did he dream, what worlds did he find?
A book full of stars, twinkling so bright,
Reach out and touch, then fly to the light!

Grandma is gone; father's gone too,
They drift in the heavens, they see me with you.
I tell of my journey, starting out poor,
It began in the kitchen and led out the door!

As of the year 2009, Lyford, Indiana consists of a few dozen houses along old U.S. Highway 41, just east of the Wabash River and north of Terre Haute. Small green road signs mark the limits of the town. It's not much of a town, really, now that the coal mines have all closed. A vacant lot sits just north of the "Y" in the road that branches north to Rockville and west to Clinton.

I visit the old town occasionally. The stone foundation of my Grandparent's home still peeks above the grass and weeds of the vacant lot. A new house sits nearby; I don't know who lives there.

In the evening in my mind, the new house fades away, and my Grandparents' old home returns. Through the window, I see my Grandmother in the kitchen, working in the glow of a lamp that rests on the table. I hear her voice across a span of nearly sixty years. After a time, the voice fades, and I am left alone among the stones of the old foundation.

Stones

Observe the stones, like old white bones, lying on the ground,
Foundation stone, my ancient home, now scattered all around!
Stones lament: "Once we meant, the base of a house that soared,
Now it's gone, life is done, and stones remain so cold!"

Patterns past, amongst the grass, beneath an evening sky,
A memory place, a ghostly space, a voice that softly sighs!
I hear a voice, Grandma's voice; it comes from long ago,
Her words so wise, see twinkling eyes, in the lamplight glow!

"Follow dreams, there's more it seems, beyond these meager walls,
You must leave, new heights achieve, a larger world now calls!"
As she said, my life path led, far out her homely door,
I have achieved, I know she's pleased, that I'm no longer poor!

Now stones and I, 'neath open sky, remember stories told,
By lamp at night, a child's delight, old walls and love enfold!
A swirl of leaves from nearby trees, the voice now fades away,
Her spirit shares other cares, the stones and I must stay!

For I'm now old, no longer bold, I've circled back around,
To sit with stones, like old white bones, scattered on the ground!
A soft lament, her life was spent; she helped my dreams to soar,
She's long gone, and I'm alone, the stones they are so cold!

Every argument with the Lord ends the same way: the old boy always wins! Still, the arguments are worthwhile; I gain insight and I suspect that the Lord is thoroughly amused; I can imagine the twinkle in his eyes! Anyway, my last argument went as follows.

Fishin'

Bank on a pond, so sunny and warm, bugs are a-buzzin', they mean no harm;
Cane pole in hand, one end on the ground, bobber on twine, just floatin' around.

Hook has a worm, there's more in a can, old hat tipped down, bare toes in the sand;
Waitin' for bluegills, or maybe not, I'm old and I dream, in my fishin' spot!

Wrinkled and gray, but young in my soul, dreamin' away, with my fishin' pole.
Days of labor are over and done, my bones are weary; I'll rest in the sun.

Long I did strive, a-workin' for gold, now I can sit, dreamin' so bold!
Now listen up Lord, be seein' you soon, let's talk 'bout fishin' and singin' a tune!

Workin' time's long, fishin' time's short, let's turn this around, the clock to re-start!
Youth seems wasted, hot work in the sun, rather be fishin' and havin' some fun!

Then came a voice, clear as a bell, "It's the Lord a-talkin', hear me well!
I know you're tired; worked a long life; met every test; seen sorrow and strife!

Life is tough, I made it that way; man must work to appreciate play!
You'll get a reward; heaven awaits; there's a big quiet pond, past heaven's gate!

I'll sit with you soon and fish in the sun, bluegills we'll catch, and when we're done,
I'll fry'um up crisp and serve'um up hot, with salad so green and tea from a pot!

Now sit and relax, be content with your lot, soon we'll meet in a great fishin' spot!
I won't forget the promise I've made, be seein' you then, inside my gate!"

Quiet returns, bugs buzzin' again, old hat tipped down, toes in the sand.
Lord has a way of clearin' the air, fishin' in heaven, he's waitin' up there!

We'll fish for bluegills, or maybe not, really don't care; I'm content with my lot!
We'll talk and laugh; just him and me, Lord I'm a-fixin' to abide with thee!

The Holy Bible provides spiritual guidance through a wonderful set of stories. Yet these stories can be told in many ways. Read the poem that follows and see if you recognize the characters!

Ole' Coon

Ole' coon up a tall gum tree, cuz big Red chased him there,
I came runnin' fast and free, a boy with sun-streaked hair!
I see the scene so clearly, it seems just yesterday,
Ole' coon I see upon that tree, big Red a-keepin' bay!

Treed a-dozen times a-fore, but smart as paint he be,
He slipped down tree to ground, an' hid away from me!
But on that night in the dark, we spoiled for a fight,
Big Red an' me coon up a tree, what a glorious sight!

I'm comin' Red a-runnin', a-cross the woodland floor,
Gonna bring coon down an' nail his crown to the wood shed door!
Shots missed their mark cuz it wuz dark, all my shells I spent,
Dad-rat that coon he grinned too soon, cuz up that tree I went!

Found a stick for fight to pick, tree swayin' to an' fro,
In that tree just coon an' me, Red howlin' down below!
The battle raged round and round, stick, teeth an' bloody hair,
A fight to win in branches thin, up thirty feet in the air!

The fight did stop when way up top, eyes blazin' fiery red,
I swung and missed ole' coon he hissed, an' dropped down on my head!
I cursed he screamed, I lost to coon that fight for another round,
Had me there fair an' square, but he smiled an' jumped to ground!

He landed soft then turned all 'round, spoil in' for a-fight,
Red looked up, saw me stuck, an' ran clear out of sight!
Another time we'll meet an' fight, but next time I will win,
Ole' coon laughed an' then he passed into the night again!

Now I'm old my story's told, I know he's still out there,
In heaven meet old foes to greet, fight him fair an' square!
Ole' coon an' me chase up a tree, round an' round again,
He'll grin I'll cuss, oh such a fuss, we'll battle an' I will win!

Now Lord you see just how it is, can I win in heaven?
I'm tired a-chasin' ole' coon down here, just barely make a-livin'!
Now the Lord has ways just to say how he feels 'bout me,
He said: "It seems jus' like a dream, but heaven's great you'll see!"

"Now my son when you come, up to the pearly gates,
Like you perceive there is a tree; climb, cuz it be your fate!"
"Heaven waits cuz I forgive, when it's time for you to go,
Ole coon's here an' he's aware, you didn't win below!

You can fight 'bout every night, but in the end you know,
Like lamb an' lion we'll all lie down an' rest so meek and low!
When you git here I'll make it clear, ole' coon he'll grin you'll see,
Hello my son! For now you've won, cuz that ole' coon wuz me!"

Early morning: others are still asleep, the sun glows on the eastern horizon, a fire burns on the hearth, and new day waits in anticipation. It is a time for reflection and for sorting things out. It is the best time of day, especially in winter.

Morning Wind

Wind outside the window; hear its mournful sound,
Winter chill creeps to my bones, dead leaves swirl all 'round!
Early morn, a darkened room; my love stays warm in bed,
Window glows; see eastern sky; clouds with streaks of red!
Reflection time, ghostly time, my night dreams fade away,
Must make my list of things to do before I start the day.
Wistful thoughts pass window; join wind in mournful sound,
Winter chill has touched my soul; dead leaves swirl all 'round!

Duty calls and I must list each task my will to test,
Complete the chores of daily life before next nighttime rest!
Perhaps cold wind soon will end and through the clearing glass,
A soft pale light will pierce the night; I'll see a golden path!
Renewal time, a peaceful time, dark clouds will pass away,
List happy things that we might do before next fading day!
Hope will flow through window, no wind or mournful sound,
Sun will warm my trusting soul and happiness surround!

Soon you'll rise with sleepy smile and share my new insight,
We'll look through our clearing glass, and see a golden light!
Then we'll kindle candles; eyes will twinkle in their glow,
You'll snuggle close to me; I'll confide what we both know!
'Though winter's here, do not fear, just see our golden path,
The pale sunrise will touch our souls through the clearing glass!
My heart warms with thoughts of you; they fade the mournful sound,
The wind will end; we'll kiss and sigh; contentment will surround!

We'll talk about the future, when spring will come again,
We'll sip our morning coffee, and let our day begin!
We'll share great dreams of travel, in glow of candle light,
And hold a peaceful moment, forget the troubled night!
I don't know how to say it, but love 'tween you and me,
Makes each morning special, our golden path we'll see!
It warms my heart just thinking; forget the mournful sound,
The wind will fade; you will come, with happiness all 'round!

Co-workers anticipate the retirement of a friend with mixed emotions. Most everyone will miss the prospective retiree, of course. However, speculation on "why" is a game played in every workplace! Bet I know the gossip around Endeavour Elementary School!

I Have a Secret!

I have a secret! Tween you an' me,
Linda's retiring! Just wait an' see!
She finally moves up, out of fifth grade,
Now endless summer, work memories fade!

She plans travel, with Frank by her side,
Fine wine an' dining, jet planes to ride!
Really no secret, 'bout everyone knows,
Linda's retiring! An' it really shows!

I have a secret! Tween you an' me,
Maybe she's going 'cause Frank's on a spree!
Who really knows the hearts of old men?
When wifey's away, does mischief begin?

He's not home alone, that's a sure bet,
The old boy's a-roamin', he's not senile yet!
Linda's suspicious, line Frank will toe,
Frank has no secret, 'cause Linda must know!

I have a secret! Tween you an' me,
Linda's a-plannin' to travel the sea!
Cruisin' an' smoozin' an' dancin' so gay,
Thinkin' 'bout drinkin', she'll party all day!

Bet Frank will pine for peace every day,
Wistful he'll be, for home far away!
Linda will drag him from ship to the shore,
It's really no secret, Linda wants more!

I have a secret! Tween you an' me,
Linda's retiring! An' jealous I be!
She finally moves up, here we all stay,
Workin' an' teachin' while Linda does play!

But she's paid her dues for thirty-four years,
Guess she can go; we'll shed a few tears!
It's really no secret, 'bout everyone knows,
Linda's ready to play and it really shows!

Time for another change of pace: let's take a dangerous turn and talk about politicians! After all, the blather of such critters dominates the TV news and the newspapers, and we can't seem to get away from the incessant "noise!" Where do they all come from!? A careful analysis results in the following conclusions.

Politicians evolve, or more accurately stated, devolve, from normal humans. Just take a reasonably intelligent man or woman, add a slight hint of power over ordinary humans, and the process of devolution begins!

Most often, the devolution process creates one of two political subspecies. These are called "Left" and "Right." Sometimes normal humans call the Leftists "liberals" and the Rightists "conservatives." However, these terms are both misnomers. Leftists express conservative views when it suits their purpose, and Rightists occasionally support liberal causes. Both subspecies will say whatever is required to get elected to political office!

Normal humans view both political subspecies with a mixture of amusement, amazement, and bewilderment. Normal humans generally tolerate politicians, at least in this current day and age, in the United States. However, in the past, politicians have been tarred, feathered, and run out of town on a rail! Such traditions still simmer beneath the surface in many minds, especially during "peak promise season," which occurs in late October every couple of years or so. Aspiring politicians who want to begin the devolution process should be aware of such traditions and take appropriate precautions; for example, they might limit the number of outrageous promises made during the heat of their campaigns!

Politicians

In the fall they have a ball; we hear 'um quick an' quack,
Walk the street, all they greet, a-spoutin' this an' that!
Jus' see the politicians, a special breed of note,
Promise moon an' silver spoon, jus' to get our vote!

Met such a man the other day, he was so fine sincere,
"Hello my friend! Just shake my hand! I'm for your interests dear!
Good works I'll do! Spend for you! Calm your every fear,
I'll cut your tax! Just hear my facts!" An' I heard him loud an' clear!

"I'm true and blue! I'm all for you! But I need your vote,
Now the other guy, he's slick and sly; he'll sink our common boat!
There's no hitch; I'll tax the rich, for you a golden door!"
He sounded good, like Robin Hood, he'll help the working poor!

"Take a stand! Save our land! Our party's all for you,
Just send a check, and make your bet, the American thing to do!"
He had his say then turned away; he smiled at someone new,
"Hello my friend! Just shake my hand! I'll work so hard for you!"

Walked down the line, an' by an' by, he repeated every word,
To great and small, one an' all, the finest speech I've heard!
Gone for now, I wonder how, he'll keep the promise made,
Will he forget when out of sight, his memory quick to fade?

But don't dismay, the very next day, his opponent fine sincere,
Walked up to me, a-smilin' free, an' I heard him loud an' clear!
"Hello my friend! Just shake my hand! I'll calm your every fear!"
Same old words, heard before: "I'm for your interests dear!"

What shall we do with politicians, jus' us common folk,
When they promise moon an' silver spoon, jus' to get our vote?
We can't hang 'um, tar or feather 'um, not this day an' age,
But we can dream 'bout a scene when truth will turn the page!

Left then right, then left again, hear the siren song! The political cycle swings from one extreme to the other; accompanied by voter enthusiasm, then waning optimism, then disillusion, then stony silence, and finally, suspicion and cynicism. Throw the rascals out! A complete cycle takes about eight years. Will politicians ever find a middle way?

Left Then Right!

Left then right, what a fight! Survey the political scene,
Right for might, left for dreams, most folks in between!
They roll their drums! They flap their gums! Enemies assail,
Can't seem to find the ties that bind and common sense prevail!

The left it seems wants only dreams, a social paradise,
The right will fight for markets, all must have free choice!
The left derides the capitalist; the right forgets the poor,
Neither sees the other's view, nor opens friendship's door!

Each must have their own way, the common good forgotten,
Common folk urged to vote; they sense that somethin's rotten!
Why don't they stop an' listen, left and right alike,
We'll get by if we simplify, an' stop this useless fight!

Jus' follow our constitution, an' keep the taxes low,
Provide for helpless orphans, a little kindness show!
Buy an' sell in freedom, but follow golden rule,
Be honest in our dealin's, it's not so hard to do!

The best laws are quite simple, so folks can understand,
Like parents teach their children, in homes across the land!
Let Congress learn from children, instead of left and right,
It might be wise to compromise, before they sleep at night!

So left and right, stop this fight! Let tranquil be the scene,
Set markets free an' kindly be, in what we do and mean!
Forget the drums, get greater sums, when we don't assail,
Seek an' find the ties that bind, let common sense prevail!

Candle, candle, golden light, show the way, provide insight! These words say, in a poet's way, what all of us know; a candle glows within! Look deep inside during special moments, and you will see. For example, I like early mornings before dawn, when the house is quiet. I light scented candles to accent the morning glow, but the true candle resides within my soul; it glows even brighter than the ones on the table! May you perceive your own lighted candle as you read the following poem!

Candle

Candle, candle burning bright, greet the morning's silver light,
Breaking, making, newborn day, drinking coffee, dawn light play!
Clearing sky, birds take wing, pass the tree tops, hear them sing,
Blue on silver, turns to gold, colors creeping, from dark to bold!
Scented candle, mixing fair, morning breezes, adds sweet flair,
Pin point stars against deep blue, winking blinking, just for you!
Your sleepy smile, soft tousled hair, just walk to me, kisses share,
Morning candle, magic wand, please hold my hand, lover's bond!

Candle, candle dancing light, grace the evening, hearts delight,
Gleaming, glowing, gold on walls, lover's shadow, romance calls!
White dining table, set for two, see elegant candle, it waits for you,
Please be seated, I'll serve our meal, savor moments, warmth we feel!
Lighted candle accents your eyes, smiles and touches, loving sighs,
Shine light on wine, feel golden glow, raise our glasses, sip it slow!
Finish dinner, now time to sit, enjoy our coffee, share gentle wit,
Evening candle, romantic light, love your eyes, twinkling bright!

Candle, candle, soft smooth light, ease the shadows of the night,
Restless sleepless, stormy eve, end the darkness, let shadows flee!
Night's dark gate, soul awaits, seeking solace, time and space,
Inside your light, meaning find, flickering flame, sooth my mind!
Gold and golden, candle glow, show the truths that I must know,
Softly gently, weave your spell, show the future, dreams foretell!
Slowly healing, find relief, calm night fears, assuage my grief,
Night time candle, glowing warm, let my mind be safe from harm!

Candle, candle, bright holy light, church on Sunday, altar white,
Giving, sharing, purest light, raise our spirits, calm life's fight!
Burdens heavy, souls are down, seek salvation, heaven's crown,
See golden symbol, light so fair, Savior listens, hears our prayers!
Solemn sermon, candle glows, words of wisdom, good Lord knows,
Praising phrasing, room grows warm, candle glows, soothing balm!
Then service over, candle stays, folks now smile, resolve their ways,
Sunday candle, high symbol fair, gives us hope, the Lord does care!

All the candles, like golden flowers, show life's meaning, mystic powers,
Just simple light, but see it flame, it glows within, for all the same!
Find life's wisdom, candle glow, burning, burning your soul will know,
Let's sit together, hold my hand, flame before us; now understand!
Morning golden, evening still, night time shadows, Sunday's thrill,
Always in us, lifelong game, guides our pathways, bright small flame!
Life has meaning and this I know, deep within us, candles glow,
Candle, candle, oh so bright, feel it burning, golden light!

Shakespeare said it best: "life is but a stage." To paraphrase the Bard, we players act our parts, and then we exit. Each of us acts out two major parts: youth and age. Youth leaps on stage, expresses soaring ideas, feels great passion, and reaches for the sky! Time tames youth, and age walks slowly on stage. Age knows that few ideas are new; passions always cool, and feet should remain firmly on the ground! Such knowledge matures into wisdom. Yet age feels wistful: oh to be young again!

September's Song

Youth and age tread life's stage, fast then slow, then wisdom sage,
Both parts cast, first then last, now quick on stage, each so fast!
Youth comes first, full of sport, peels of laughter, patience short,
Age comes last, patience fair, calmly smiles, with love to share!

Youth finds hope, bright early spring, seeks hot summer, growing things,
Nimble movements, dress in fashion, glorious flowers, and wanton passion!
Great songs to sing, spirits high, like birds on wing, now touch the sky,
Youth bursts with life, plays the game, soaring high, but time does tame!

Age finds care, sorrows call, wind feels cold, leaves now fall,
Slower walk, wrinkles show, golden sunsets, passions slow!
September's song, gentle tune, star-filled nights, silver moon,
Age bows humble, sometimes sick, time flies by, oh so quick!

Youth and age, both must pass, songs and passion cannot last,
Age now on stage, resigned to fates, exit looms, judgment waits!
One last glass of cool sweet wine, smile again, speak final line,
Time soon over, but with age, wisdom shows, then walks off stage!

The stage lights dim; all should know; the end approaches, in evening glow! We've played our parts, youth now past, age is here, make moments last! Aged lovers smile, as lovers must, then slowly exit, and come to dust! Heaven waits for those who trust, and share the faith, as share we must! Love will last, with patience wait; we'll meet on stage, past heaven's gate!

5. TRAVELS WITH LINDA

Linda excites and amuses me, and she warms my old heart! We walk our golden path; we laugh and love; we anticipate, and we plan. She brings meaning to my life!

We are fortunate in our autumn years, we are relatively affluent. We can afford to travel. Life is good!

Linda and I love to plan trips; anticipation is half the fun! (Well, maybe a third.) Anyway, as long as we can, we will travel to new places, enjoy the views, eat at fine restaurants, and sip good wine. Why not? Linda worked for thirty-four years; I worked forty-five, and we saved our money. It's time to play!

Next Trip!

Planning, planning, next trip 'round, to the moon or on the ground,
Read travel books in fireside nooks, our dreams will soar unbound!
You plan with me and we'll just see, which great new trip ranks best,
Shall we go here, there or everywhere? Let's put each trip to test!
Now bright white moon in early June, it sounds just great to me,
See a fantastic view! It's all so new! Shall we fly on up and see?
But moon we go, we may miss the show, on earth this next July,
Oh, dad-rat! We can't do that! So we'll just grow wings and fly!

Planning, planning, new trips found, to the stars or just around,
Flying here and there, just everywhere! So many choices found!
It's all so grand, please hold my hand! We'll see and go and love,
As dreamers sail, our hearts will prevail, do trips outlined above!
This spring on earth, view re-birth; flowers and new green leaves,
It's all so new! See sparkling dew! A springtime spell that weaves!
If spring we go, might miss the show, of summer 'round the corner,
So we'll just pick, spring flowers so slick, and carry on into summer!

Planning, planning, fall trip found, to the mountains or just around,
Drive here and there, go everywhere; see colors: red, gold and brown!
Oh, what a view, 'neath sky so blue! See snow on high mountain crest,
Feel sunshine glowing, leaves are blowing, soon winter snow will test,
If fall we go, then we will know, that cold winter creeps close behind,
So we'll bundle up, hold hot coffee cup, and frost we'll never mind!
Dreams of awe, cold freeze then thaw, soon skiers swish down hill,
Feel crystal snow, see moonlight glow, dark trees hold night so still!

Planning, planning, trips we found, moon or season, they come 'round,
With longing looks, view picture books, our dreams come true somehow!
You with me, we'll go and see, where the best picture views are found,
They're each so fair! We'll go everywhere! Let travel trumpets sound!
Now we're in thrall, having a ball! From tall mountains to blue sea,
A wonderful view, but it's just really you that I truly want to see!
If great trips we go, you're the show, on moon, on earth, in sky,
So hold my hand and understand, you make the trips soar high!

After many years of business travel, I have learned to pack; I use one medium-sized travel bag and my briefcase. In general, this is enough for about a week on the road, two weeks in a pinch. On the other hand, until we got married in 2007, Linda had not traveled much (school teachers are chained to their desks, or so Linda said). It is fun to watch her pack for one of our vacations. The packing process can take up to two weeks each trip!

Linda is a-Packin'!

Packin's a pleasure not to be missed,
Vacation a-comin', look at her list!
She's all in a tizzy, get ready to play,
Dozens of outfits, change twice a day!

One suitcase for me, five for the wife,
Good thing we're goin' for only six nights!
She needs more suitcases, five isn't enough,
She'll need a truck to haul all this stuff!

Check colors for match, detail gets caught,
Blouse doesn't match last sweater she bought.
Excuse for more shopping, new stuff to pack,
Four blouses one coat, right off the rack!

Still in a tizzy, checkin' her list,
Bet she forgot her hairspray mist!
Bound to be somethin' not packed in a fuss,
Shop when she gets there, sundries and such.

I'll load the car, stackin' her things,
I'm prepared, car has overload springs!
Packin's the game, just bear it and grin,
Pack it and stack it, just can't win!

It may be a surprise to youngsters, but old folks do not always sit in rocking chairs, tell stories of days gone by, and wait patiently for the kids and grandkids to visit! We have plans and dreams, and we are ready to play!

Our Turn!

Autumn is here, what's sown we reap,
Our time to enjoy, before winter's sleep!
Interest to spend from money we earned,
Let's go play, because it's our turn!

Kids grown up, we've earned some rest,
Good times and sorrows, met every test!
Now we're alone, with money we earned,
Let's enjoy quiet, because it's our turn!

Travel by limo, or first class jet,
Cruise ship sails, our cares to forget!
Fine dining and shopping, see lovely sights,
Sunshine by day, stars gleam at night!

Maitre 'd greets us, we're special guests,
Table for two, dressed in our best!
Hand in hand, we talk for awhile,
Fine wine is served, the sommelier smiles.

Waiters attend us, soft music floats by
Dance after dinner, laugh as we glide!
Old but hale, with money we earned,
Dance and be glad, because it's our turn!

Shopkeepers smile, we walk through the door,
Know what we like, been here before!
Clothes that are tailored, jewelry that glows,
Shopping for fun, we savor it slow!

The tab we pay, our wants we fulfill,
Long as we're careful, no worries on bills!
Shop 'til we drop, money we earned,
Laces and silks, because it's our turn!

Afternoon wanes, we walk hand in hand,
Along a smooth path, gold lights the land!
I tell of my love, you give me a smile,
Eyes meet and sparkle, kiss for awhile.

Sunset aglow, see glorious sight,
Love 'til the end, then walk to the night.
We worked and saved, let's spend what we earned,
Play and be glad, because it's our turn!

Travel by car across the country provides opportunities for insight into the human condition. Small towns just off the highway have characters with poignant stories; if we choose to observe and perhaps listen.

Old Man at the Bar

Long road, small town, cold winter's day,
Found an old inn along the highway.
Rooms for guests above the main floor,
Bar and grill, inside the door.

Quick in from the wind, we sat near the bar,
Hot meal and coffee, warm by the fire.
Simple and light, then back on the road,
Continue our travels, out in the cold.

Relax with our food, cozy and warm,
Look 'round the place, shabby and worn.
Locals at bar, drinks in their hands,
Mostly in pairs, but one single old man.

Farm boots and jeans, weathered old hat,
Grey and sad, he slumped as he sat.
"Howdy!" he said, as we looked his way,
We nodded and smiled, then looked away.

He looked for awhile, then back to his drink,
Our message was clear; he wouldn't insist.
He turned to the locals, they moved down the bar,
They wouldn't listen, heard it before.

Old man bored them, even when sober,
Long sad story, told many times over.
He then talked to himself, rambled and sighed,
Words indistinct, tears in his eyes.

It must have been tragic, the story he told,
That day in the bar, refuge from cold.
Was there a woman, lost long ago?
We chose not to listen, so we'll never know.

Daylight waned, we finished our meal,
The old man remained, his voice now still.
Door opened wide, a silhouette loomed,
Young man paused; then walked in the room.

He stood by the bar, observed the old man,
Smiling he said: "Ready to go, Sam?"
The old man nodded, smiled in return,
No words came, eyes watered and burned.

Shaky he rose; he had been there awhile,
Young man steadied his arm with a smile.
Old and young, they walked through the door,
Wind blew in, snow swirled on the floor.

We sat silent, time stood so still,
Finished our coffee; paid up our bill.
Wind blew cold as we walked in the night,
Stars up above, twinkling and bright.

It must have been tragic, the story he told,
Old man at the bar, refuge from cold.
Was there a woman, lost long ago?
We chose not to listen, so we'll never know!

Ghosts from the past walk the trails that we still follow today. Turn off the car radio; keep your eyes on the road and the car between the white lines, and let your mind roam free!

Santa Fe Trail!

Long day's travel, straight I-25, along wagon ruts, the past comes alive!
It's the Santa Fe Trail, dimly I see, ghosts from the past, looking through me.

They may see me, spirits from past, but I'm just a dream, a future through glass!
Yet we connect, seems a strange thing, romance in my soul, memories have wings.

I'm bored and restless, car hums along, minutes turn hours, hear a faint song!
A song of times when wagons hauled freight, out on the trail, hooves steady gait.

"Move along ox! Pull all your might! No rest this day, exhaustion tonight!
Shade is a dream! Pray for some rain! Fill the dry washes, thirsty I am!

At home in Missouri signed on the line, gold in Santa Fe, four months hard times!
Senoritas a-waitin' at trail's long end, dark hair and eyes, lovely soft skin!

Bath and a shave, traveler's delight, raw whiskey and lovin', oh what a night!
Meantime the smell, ox dung and sweat, scratchy dry throat, death a good bet!

Danger abounds, joints feel the pain, scurvy and rattlesnakes, heat on the plain!
Ute and Cheyenne, trails we must cross, they want our goods, lives will be lost.

This land is theirs, intruders we be, I'd do the same, trade places with me!
Pole star is north, pass is southwest, long past Canadian, water and rest.

Past Trinidad village, snake through the pass, Santa Fe distant, see lights at last!
Trail ends soon, live through this day, whiskey and lovin', ahead for our stay!"

Song fades away, as road takes a turn, car over pass, sun sets in gloom.
Ghosts have vanished, yet memories remain, days on the trail, all just a dream?

Santa Fe gleams, modern town waits, hotel on the Plaza, soft bed and new fates.
It seemed so real, not just a dream, ghosts from the past, singing to me!

I'll dream tonight, may they return, wagons and oxen, grim men, burning sun!
Romance my soul, the past my domain, on Santa Fe trail, spirits remain!

Holidays are often lonely for older people. The holiday dawns, and we wait for the phone to ring. When it does, we hear the voices of our adult children.

The voices are stilted but cheerful, conversations usually center on the weather (it's always too hot or too cold, we are expecting snow, etcetera); they always ask how we are doing (they want to hear: "we are doing fine!"); we ask about how the grandkids are doing in school (they are always getting all A's and B's, girls are signed up for dance lessons, boys for some sport, and so on).

Grandchildren are put on the phone by Mom and Dad, and it's easy to discern that they have been coached on what to say. The grandkids always say "thank you for the great present," and occasionally they actually remember what they got from Grandma and Grandpa.

After a short conversation with the grandkids, the phone is turned over to Mom or Dad. As the conversation draws to a close, there is usually an ending with some version of "we really must get together sometime." For some of us, there is an alternative holiday!

Two This Christmas

Just two this Christmas, we'll travel this year,
Fine wine and roses, sweet holiday cheer!
Our families have plans; we're on our own,
So follow the sun, two walk alone.

Old partners now gone, death took its toll,
Winter is near, the world turns cold.
We found each other, to hold for awhile,
You laugh at my jokes, I treasure your smile!

Now that we're old, quiet is good,
The young want action, restless their mood.
We bore them, they disturb us,
Go south, stay warm, avoid the fuss!

The choice we made, disturbing to some,
Along our new path, families won't come.
Sad in some ways, but we're on our own,
We'll follow the sun, two walk alone!

Cars have personalities that mirror our own. Even old folks can laugh, feel free, and experience joy; the wind blows our gray hair, and we speed down the highway! Hey Linda, little Red is ready to go again!

Our Little Red

Car trip for us, sun brightly glows,
Start Little Red, let's hit the road!
Named for color, but now that it's said,
A car with an attitude, our Little Red!

Spiffy and sleek, luxury to please,
Soft golden pinstripes, V8 for speed!
Fine leather seats and buttons galore,
Don't know them all, but we can explore!

We'll flip a coin, who drives today?
Sharing is tough, Red wants to play!
I win the toss, but you're by my side,
Out on the road, just two for a ride!

Red hums along, a song we share,
I hold your hand, to show that I care.
Freedom to roam, like birds on the wing,
Matching Red's tune, happy hearts sing!

Red cost a bundle, but such fun to drive,
Off to the country, our time has arrived!
Folks wave as we pass, we smile in return,
Two old fogies, with money we earned!

Kids think we're nuts, we really don't care,
Laughing out loud, no time to spare!
Out on the road, just you and me dear,
Red wants to play, I'll shift to high gear!

Follow the highway, the country flies by,
Dark clouds gather but you're by my side!
Your eyes twinkle; love your sweet smile,
As long as we can, we'll travel in style!

Red understands, she steers through the storm,
We snuggle inside, cozy and warm!
The storm will end, as we glide along,
Golden our sunset, contentment our song!

Airports are a pain in the butt: long lines, uncomfortable seats, endless concourses, delays and overpriced food. However, little things provide amusement, even a simple sandwich!

Dividing the Sandwich

A quickie lunch at airport café,
Time is short, we cannot stay.
Fast food's the ticket, just grab a bite,
Down the hatch, then catch the next flight!

Just one sandwich for us to share,
Fries and a coke, all standard fare.
Waitress was prompt, gave sandwich to you,
You grabbed a knife and cut it in two.

The trouble was the meat inside,
Filled half the bun before the divide!
You cut the sandwich and gave me my share,
You got meat, my bun was bare!

You wolfed yours down, blink of an eye,
I chewed my bun and breathed a sigh!
You shared the fries, I got two,
Just wait 'til next time, I'll share with you!

When it comes to shopping, men and women arrive from different planets! A man will spend twenty dollars for a ten dollar item he really needs. On the other hand, a woman will spend ten dollars for a twenty dollar item she might need, someday, maybe! Men clearly need lessons on how to shop. Most women are happy to oblige!

Shopping Lesson

Shop on vacation, won't spend too much,
The folks at home want trinkets and such!
Just budget one hundred, for Linda and me,
Walk through the stores, mild shopping spree!

Found trinkets on sale, four items she spies,
Take fifty percent off the original price!
Just fifty bucks each, the total's two hundred.
"But Linda!" said I: "Our budget's one hundred!"

Then Linda explained: "It's easy to see,
I'm saving money on our shopping spree!"
"The cost was four hundred, now it's half price,
So I saved two hundred, isn't that nice?"

Bought the four items, spend all our cash,
One hundred from budget, plus my secret stash!
Befuddled and muddled, all logic's been waived,
Still trying to find the money we saved!

I could write pages on the delight women find in clipping and shopping with coupons. However, Linda is observing, so discretion is the better part of valor!

Those of us who grew up on the farm remember getting up at "Zero dark thirty" and heading to the barn. We milked the cows, fed the chickens, cleaned out the barn, and so on. Getting out of bed before dawn every day, good weather or bad, with no holidays, caused habits and attitudes to form that stayed with us, even after we moved to the city. We still get out of bed at "Zero dark thirty," at home or even on vacation. Kids who grew up in town formed different habits!

In our old age, it's fun to harass the sleeping spouse who grew up in town. It's almost daybreak: time to get out of bed!

Get Out of Bed!

Are you out of bed yet? Good heavens!
The cows are all milked, the chickens are fed,
And you, lazy bones, are still in bed!

New worlds to conquer, the night is long dead,
The birds are chirping, they let it be said,
Your presence is wanted, but you're still in bed!

Breakfast is ready, table's all spread,
Coffee's a-waitin' there's butter and bread,
If you want any, then get out of bed!

Your head under pillow, eyes blurry and red,
Too much night life, so fuzzy your head,
So my foot to your butt, now get out of bed!

Linda and I both grew to adulthood in the Midwest: Iowa for Linda and Indiana for yours truly. Road trips back to our roots bring nostalgia and moments to reflect on how far we have journeyed in body and soul.

On our last trip "home," we stayed in bed and breakfast inns: first in Maquoketa, Iowa and then in Terre Haute, Indiana. Linda still knows half the people in Maquoketa, including the owners of Squiers Manor Inn.

I can't claim the same for Terre Haute, but I do know the countryside, the towns and the farms from Terre Haute south to Sullivan, and from the Wabash to Indianapolis. Sycamore Farm Inn provided a pleasant base for our Indiana visit. Linda and I walked the land and she was introduced to my "Wind Grass Hill." Squiers and Sycamore provided places to reminisce and to write.

Squiers Manor rests on a quiet street in Maquoketa. Nearby houses have white painted wood siding, large front porches, bluegrass lawns and two stories. Most are surrounded by large trees: maple and oak mostly, but even a few American elms. All are well-maintained; they are like a time capsule from a century ago.

Squiers has a similar style, except that reddish bricks have been used instead of painted wood. It is surrounded by a wrought iron fence. In its heyday one hundred years ago, it was the finest house in the neighborhood, owned by the wealthy Squiers family. Now it sits as a well-kept dowager, peacefully providing a warm, welcoming retreat for a few visitors at a time. Inside, most rooms are paneled in warm rich butternut wood. There are several fireplaces with carved wood mantles. The dining room has a crystal chandelier. The four bedrooms each have a separate bathroom; ours was original when the house was built. It is a most comfortable inn!

Squiers Manor

Last morning at Squiers, Midwest town,
Time stands still, memories abound.
Remember the days, children at play,
So long, long ago, seems yesterday!

We walk this morning, past green lawns,
Summer breeze sighs, birds greet the dawn.
Street of old homes, white above grass,
Folks fetch their papers, wave as we pass.

Walk down the block then back to Squiers gate,
Up wooden steps, our breakfast awaits.
Coffee smells good, hot biscuits and eggs,
Fresh fruit and juice, sip to the dregs.

Finish our breakfast, time to check out,
Hostess is kind, she bustles about.
Breeze touches trees, soft sighing sound,
Bags to the car, roll windows down.

Drive down the street, slowly through town,
Clock starts again, yet memories abound.
Old and new friends, so mellow our stay,
Squiers fades from view, as we drive away.

Have you ever been to an Entmoot? I have! In Iowa, they are called "family gatherings." For those of you who have read J.R.R. Tolkien's "Lord of the Rings," you may remember the "Entmoot" in the book "The Two Towers." As Tolkien might have said: "Ents are as different from each other as an oak is from an elm tree, but the eyes now, they are the same…"

An Entmoot is a gathering of Ents. To paraphrase Tolkien: "As soon as the whole company (of Ents) assembles in a wide circle, a curious and unintelligible (to outsiders) conversation begins. The Ents begin to murmur slowly: first one joins and then another, until they are all chanting together in a long rising and falling rhythm, now louder on one side of the circle, now dying away there and rising to a great boom on the other side."

In the Midwest, family gatherings are like Entmoots. All the relatives gather at someone's home and sit on chairs in somewhat of a circle, often on a big screened back porch, or if the weather's good and the bugs don't come out, on a patio adjacent to a big green yard. There are big folks and little folks, old and young, aunts, uncles, and cousins to the ninth degree. Everyone (except one or two outsiders who may be visiting) knows the family history at least as far back as the eldest person present. Once gathered, the conversations begin, usually several at a time, and folks move in and out of each conversation as smoothly as if they know the precise content of each separate conversation, all at the same time! Last Spring, Linda and I visited her family in Iowa. The following poem tells the story of the visit and the Iowa Entmoot!

Home Town Relations!

Midst Iowa hills, broad rivers, small rills, past wheat an' lots of tall corn,
Visit Zwingle becuz, that's near where it wuz, Linda was long ago born!
Past crossroads near town, road winds 'round, drivin' most of the morn,
'Bout fifteen mile, Maquoketa style; pass tractors but don't honk the horn!
"Zwingle's nor-east, but LaMotte's due east, don't miss the little road sign,
Jus' past the old mill, then over the hill, turn left at the fork! We'll be fine!"
Frank knows Indiana, but Iowa's grander, bigger farms an' fewer tall trees,
Jus' drive a bit slower; don't get pulled over; Cousin Bob wuz Sheriff you see!

Arrived in Zwingle, met Dennis an' Peggy; drove back to Maquoketa 'bout four,
Know Marilyn an' Cindy are fryin' up chicken; old Al's jus' a-pacin' the floor!
Now Linda's relations all comin'; we gotta be runnin'; supper will surely be ready,
For Betty an' Bill, Mary, Aunt Phyll, Bev an' John, an' Craig an' the other Peggy!
Bet everyone's a-waitin' an' all surely debatin'; who's the new guy called Frank?
Who did Linda hook up with, real or jus' myth? We'll find out an' then pull rank!
When Linda arrives, this buzzin' beehive will turn silent; all are jus' waitin' to see,
Now what does Frank do? Is he like me an' you? He has beard! How tall will he be?

Linda shows at door, with Frank in tow, the cousins are all sittin' an' a-waitin',
All 'round profusion, it's all so confusin', then introductions start conversation,
Not one but four, or maybe there's more! 'Round an' 'round goes the debatin',
So many questions all asked, re-visitin' the past, jus' who is related to whom?
"You know old Junior, he no longer lives here; he lives down Kansas City way!"
"Yes, but he has a son, some business he runs, doin' well, I heard Junior say!"
"Now old Uncle Bob, it makes your heart sob; he has medical problems you see!"
An' while one debate shares Uncle Bob's fate, Bev starts debate two on a spree!

Phyll joins the third: "Someone jus' heard; a friend in Dubuque moved away!"
Now in an' all 'round, a soft chattering sound, the voices they go higher in play!
It's like an' orchestra sans the conductor, there's so much sound in one room,
Yet insiders know, how the threads go, the whats-its an' whose-its an' whom!
Then a question is asked, 'bout Frank's past: "Frank! Jus' what do you do?"
Silence! All talk stops! Hear a pin drop! Then eyes focus on Frank all anew!
Frank jus' said: "'fore Linda an' I wed, I worked in science; now I'm retired!"
Silence again! Poor Frank can't win! "But Frank! For what were you hired?"

Poor old Frank! Prospects jus' sank! He said somethin' 'bout lasers an' moon,
But it didn't matter; they resumed chatter; all 'round an' a-round in the room!
Finally Marilyn called: "Supper!" That was a winner; put pounds on to linger,
An' Linda jus' laughed, re-visit her past, in Maquoketa, Dubuque, an' Zwingle!
It's so good to be home! Pause as we roam! Makes heart feel snug an' so warm,
Jus' home for soft thrills, in old Iowa hills, walked near the wheat and tall corn,
Everyone's so friendly, relations unending! Good folks straight from the farm!
Our road winds 'round, but we visit home town, a place with welcome so warm!

Sycamore Farm was once just that, a farm on the outskirts of Terre Haute. Now the acreage has been sold, but the house and barn remain on about four or five acres. The house and barn reside amid a grove of white oak and maple trees. The old barn has been re-modeled to provide a space for social functions. The house itself is a typical Midwestern two-story farmhouse, with white paint and dark gray trim. Inside, the main entrance is spacious and beautifully decorated in "country style." A rich, carved wooden stairway leads up at the back of the entryway. Our bedroom and bath were upstairs; both decorated in country style. The four poster bed had lovely comforters and pillows; it swallowed us up in luxurious comfort. Windows on two sides of the bedroom gave us views of trees and the barn. There was no sign of neighbors or the city. Outside, squirrels scampered about, and robins performed their timeless ritual of worm hunting in the bluegrass yard. It is a beautiful place!

Sycamore Farm

Sycamore Farm with old shingle roof,
Near a red barn, no sound of a hoof.
Old inn waits, white with gray trim,
Hides among trees, leaves green and dim.

Turn in the lane, stones line the way,
Host at the door, so glad we can stay.
Shows us our room, with four poster bed,
Flowers in white vase, fresh roses deep red.

Butternut wood trims out our room,
It glows so mellow, reminds us of home.
A home lost in time, so long ago,
Memories drift, in evening glow.

Gladly to bed, softly touch night,
Wake in the morning when robins take flight.
Night dreams pass, then slowly awake,
Dim light through window, greet the daybreak!

Rise with the sun, no hurry, slow time,
Light from kitchen, coffee smells fine!
Wash face, get dressed, then walk down the stairs,
Innkeeper greets us, breakfast prepared.

Savor our coffee, must face the day,
Our road travels on; we cannot stay.
Drive out the lane, the Innkeeper waves,
Fresh and rested, good memories made!

The old family farm belongs to other folks now. Still, I visit when I can. My parents and grandparents rest in nearby cemeteries. The old country lane that passes by the farm is much the same as it was when I was a boy. I like walking down the lane, across the bridge over the creek, and up to the old farm. I remember a rainy summer afternoon, not so long ago. Linda, perhaps we can walk the old lane together someday soon!

Old Country Lane

Old country lane, soft dappled shade, high oak trees, leaves overlaid,
Promise of rain, clouds puffy and gray, cool summer breeze, as afternoon fades!
Soothing my spirit, fond memories found, been here before, now circled around,
Returned to the country, back on home ground, soul to restore, lost and now found!
Fortune I gained, from seeking so bold, scaled all the heights, but now that I'm old,
Refresh in the rain, feel the drops cold, as I walk down the lane, back to the fold!

Past fields of corn, wheat and soybeans, pastures with blossoms, white against green,
Here I was born, learned what life means, then went away, world not what it seems!
Restore my hurt spirit, let truths be re-found, been here before, now circled around,
Returned to the country, fertile the ground, seek peace once more, lost and now found!
More to be gained by walking old road, than scaling the heights in cities with gold,
Feel soft cool rain, refreshing enfold, washing my spirit, on old country road!

Walk down the lane, rain patters glade, passing through leaves, high overlaid,
Feel the cool rain, my spirit re-made; wash away time, old city life fades!
Renewing my spirit, life will re-bound, been here before, now circled around,
Returned to the country, old sight and sound, peace once more, lost but now found!
Soft rain in the lane, healing my hurt, more than cool water, feel the re-birth,
Fortune regained, old truths re-assert, soul has renewed, here close to the earth!

Parke County Indiana hosts thirty old covered bridges, most still in daily use. At one time, there were over fifty. Over the past one hundred or so years, some have been lost to natural disasters and arson, while other were deliberately dismantled, before the days of preservation.

I was born in Clinton, Indiana, just across the Wabash River from Lyford, a crossroads town in Parke County. My grandparents lived in Lyford, and my Dad moved our family back to the old homestead after my Grandmother passed away. Parke County was a special place for a small boy. Even after a span of over sixty years, I still know the hillsides, the bottom lands, the creeks, the old cabins, and the old covered bridges!

Amish farms and buggies, the Wabash River, preserved small towns like Lyford, Rosedale and Billy Creek, places like Sugar Creek and Big and Little Raccoon Creeks, and of course, the covered bridges, provide a bucolic framework for a special, folksy way of life. When I visit the Parke County countryside, I go back in time. Sometimes, when I'm far away, I miss it so!

Old Covered Bridge

A covered bridge just down Oak Ridge, it crosses Sugar Creek,
Let's park our car; it's not very far; just a peaceful path I seek!
Full sixty years, love and tears, since I passed this sunny glade,
Small country boy, so full of joy, when on this bridge I played!

My father an' my two sisters, an' our Mom was with us too,
Kids pranced on down; we fooled around, water clean an' cool!
Adults laughed; us kids just splashed; we washed away our grime,
Then Dad unpacked some paper sacks, for a picnic supper time!

Then Mom said: "You-all need fed! I brought a watermelon!
There's fresh sun tea for you an' me; I got at least a gallon!
Got chicken legs an' deviled eggs, an' store-bought 'tater chips,
Got strawberries, pears an' cherries, an' thick cream we can dip!"

An' eat we did, then all us kids, we played by stream 'til night,
Dad an' Mom talked an' watched, in summer's fading light!
Dad an' Mom are now both gone; my sisters have moved away,
Now we walk, with not much talk; my mind in memories stray!

Oak Ridge an' bridge remember, but now under a cloudy sky,
The summer day I played away, an' the sun was riding high!
Now walk with me; I'm glad you see; hold my hand an' know,
This old country boy, in simple joy, walks in memories glow!

Back in Indiana, folks place you in the scheme of things by making connections to your local family history. Old farmsteads and all the little towns and crossroad communities have family names that have continued for nearly two hundred years. Your place in the world is defined by who married who, cousins two and three times removed, grandparents and siblings, and where you lived and when. Once the local folks find out that you have local relatives, the quiz begins. You can also bet with certainty that everyone for miles around will soon know that you are back in town! What a wonderful way to get re-acquainted with "home!"

Gas and Go Fine Dining

Midst rolling hills, past old windmills, small farms and somber woods,
Near Turkey Run, feel noonday sun, see the Hoosier neighborhoods!
A hot summer day, along the old highway, it's time for lunch and gas,
Found white clapboard store, old screen door, cars parked on the grass!
See the weathered sign, Come in and Dine! Enjoy our country fixin's,
We got our gas, parked on the grass, and walked in toward the kitchen!
Passed through the store, clean concrete floor, tables scattered 'round,
Folks a-sittin', coffee sippin', no voices, jus' clock with ticking sound!
Some kids in jeans from modest means, some old folks here and yon,
New in town, they stared and frowned, they knew we'd soon be gone!

Saw the grizzled cook; he gave us a look; he peered over his bifocals,
We nervous smiled, he broadly smiled; he could tell we weren't locals!
"Howdy folks! Want burgers and cokes? An' jus' so I don't get bored,
There's liver and fries, choice of sides, an' more on the menu board!
Got biscuits fixin' 'long with chicken, mashed 'taters an' green beans,
The milk gravy's hot, it'll hit the spot; meal comes with garden greens!
We got cakes and pies, before your eyes, on the counter jus' over there,
The hot coffee's free, so's the ice tea, 'long with your luncheon fare!
So what'll it be? Iff'n it wuz me, I'd give a try on the chicken dinner,
But now you-all decide, be it baked or fried, it's sure to be a winner!"

We looked all 'round, the menu found, a white board with printed entries,
The cook did stand, with spoon in hand, while we pondered all the entrées!
Knew what's best here, friendly gesture: "Can we have two chicken dinners?"
Cook's smile got wider, he found two platters, turned up the stove to simmer!
We looked all 'round, and then we found, a table by the ice cream cooler,
Then a little boy with a small stuffed toy, he stared from a nearby stroller!
We smiled and said: "Hey!" But he turned away; he hid his big blue eyes,
Then his Mom looked up, past coffee cup, said: "He's jus' a little bit shy!
He's jus' turned two and you-all are new, or he'd talk off both your ears!"
We laughed and I did say: "It's OK, but I used to live in a farmhouse near!"

A man turned our way, heard him say: "Have folks that live 'round here?"
"Why, 'course I do: I have sisters two; they live south of old Clinton near!
One's a Campbell, the other's a Sweeney!" Then smiles from folks did flow,
"I know old Jim! You visitin' him?" "No, Jim's my sister's brother-in-law!"
"Well I'll be darned! Old Jim had the farm; jus' down the road from us!
What's your name? It's now so plain! You look jus' like old man Gus!"
"Old Gus Blackburn? Well, I'll be dern! Old Gus was my Grandfather!
I'm young Frank, my wife here's Linda, you may have known my father!"
"Why yes! I knew old Frank! Jus' let me think! You folks lived near Lyford?"
"Why yes we did! I wuz then jus' a kid! We moved on down near Lewis!"

We talked and talked, and Linda laughed, she's also a small town girl,
Jus' plain folks way to pass the day, and make connections in a swirl!
The fried chicken served, praise well-deserved, fine dining country style,
Jus' briefly home, why did we roam? Good food, new friends, no guile!
Same names and places, with familiar faces, jus' younger versions know,
The eyes remain, they're jus' the same, as they were so long, so long ago!
A shy little boy brought all such joy, when he blinked at us and stared,
He broke the ice; we met folks so nice; we talked; we heard; we shared!
As the sun moved low, we had to go; we said fond goodbyes mid smiles,
We had gas and go fine dining, with plain talkin' Hoosier style!

Many small Midwestern towns seem to be dying. In some instances, the process has been going on for nearly half a century. Stores on Main Street have closed; vacant display windows stare out like empty eye sockets in forlorn red brick skeletons. Once beautiful, classic homes on shady streets now show faded paint; they desperately need repairs. Neighborhood schools have consolidated due to lack of students; empty school buildings now have pigeons for occupants.

There were many causes. Some towns grew up around coal mines, most Midwest mines have closed as the easily accessible coal petered out. Railroad towns dried up because rail passenger service faded along with the advent of the interstate highway system and modern car and airline travel. Trucks took over much of the rail freight transportation. Old line textile factories and other manufacturing jobs moved overseas due to cheaper labor. In general, times changed, and people moved away.

For years, young people were the major export for many towns; they headed to big cities and suburbs to find jobs. Most residents that remained were old pensioners, including many widows with little to do except remember the old days.

Yet there appears to be new hope for some towns; a few core jobs are returning; local governments have offered tax incentives and a ready pool of workers for small factories and businesses. Some towns along interstate highways have developed thriving businesses that service highway travelers and truckers. New agriculture-based activities have increased along with modern, mechanized farms. In some places, thriving tourist businesses have sprung up; the Midwest has many scenic and historic places. Also, baby boomer retirees from the big cities have started to trickle back to the simpler, less expensive towns where they have roots. Most promising of all, many young people have re-discovered small town America, and some are returning to raise families! I visited my old home town last summer, and I have reason for hope!

The Return

Midwestern town, all tumble down, old house at eight-forty South Main,
See faded pale colors, unhinged shutters; see cracks in old window pane!
Brambles and leaves, weathered roof eaves, weeds in an overgrown lawn,
See the broken gate path, with pieces of glass, mixed in the mud all brown!

Old trees need pruning; yard needs fencing, house needs painting and care,
Power line droops low from old utility pole, front porch all empty and bare!
The roof shows sag; a brown paper bag blows across trash littered ground,
All windows opaque, dust lines the glaze, no laughter, no children, no sound!

Pale light shines, behind drawn blinds, a sound from the kitchen back door,
An old woman waits, for her near certain fate, to join with those gone before!
Old life dimly glows, and town clearly shows, days of laughter have all passed,
The house like the town, wears a sad frown, no future, all faded; can't last!

But dawn light rises, light touches horizon, the shadows now fade to the west,
A young man stands, has work-hardened hands, on street as night goes to rest!
He observes the sad scene, and he has a dream, of a town with laughter again,
He knows how to re-build, his dream be fulfilled, new life in old town begin!

The man turns 'round, hears a car door sound, young woman walks to his side,
They hold warm hands; the bold dream expands; their child now grows inside!
They'll work together, things will get better, a young couple finding their roots,
Then old woman at door, her life may restore, she smiles and care lines smooth!

Restore faded pale colors, fix broken old shutters; replace the cracked window pane,
Plant flowers for spring showers; hear laughter from children; let new life start again!
More young couples may see, how good life can be; away from big city bright lights,
Midwest town, re-build from the ground; start with house at eight-forty South Main!

Trips back to Indiana bring moments for quiet reflection. Sometimes I go for real; more often I visit in my dreams. Last night as I dreamed, I visited a quiet country pasture at night. Such visits bring peace to a troubled soul. I took a walk in the moonlight, and then sat in the grass. I remained quiet, and heard and felt my own heart beating, pumping, resonating to nature's rhythm. After a time, soft, almost imperceptible sounds echoed around me in the grass. Listen!

Small Creatures

When the moon in the evening rose up in the east,
The fields glowed in soft light, a pasture at peace!
No breeze stirred the trees, no day's serenade,
When silver soft moonlight caused colors to fade!

When shadows flowed gently from east to the west,
Small creatures of night peered out from each nest!
Heard sounds in the grasses, from tiny quick feet,
When night's small creatures came out to eat!

When rustles and peeps rose up from the ground,
Ears picked out places where creatures were found!
Saw amber eyes glowing, in fur faces delight,
When moonlight reflected on eyes in the night!

When small tummies filled, sounds quieted down,
The white moon rose higher, stars formed a crown!
No movement in grasses, each creature did rest,
When midnight approached, safe in each nest!

When all sounds had ended, I walked to my door,
My footsteps pressed gently on nature's soft floor!
Did eyes of small creatures look and then wonder,
When I left their pasture and went to my slumber?

When moon passed zenith at doorstep turned 'round,
All shadows to nothing, soft moonlight, no sound!
Our lives briefly touched, small creatures and me,
When the moon in the evening rose up in the east!

Vacations and golf go together. Old country folks like Linda and I often derisively refer to golf as "cow pasture pool," and so on. Still, we play as often as we can! Golf is fun (if not taken too seriously), good exercise (even from a golf cart), and can be played by almost anyone (however poorly). Have a good game!

Golf!

Arrive at the club house, hot ready to play,
Drive a few range balls to start up the day!
Whack 'em and hack 'em, that's how it's done,
Cow pasture pool, great fun in the sun!

Finished a bucket, tee master announces,
Two-some to play, good luck on the bounces!
Jitters and titters, hope no one's looking,
Tee it up high, don't slice it or hook it!

Knees locked, arms stiff, check out the wind,
Address the ball: "Ball, please be my friend!"
Spot behind ball, now just concentrate,
Swing hard, good Lord, let it go straight!

Not too bad, the first shot did go,
Edge of the rough, 'bout one-sixty or so!
Three iron or five iron, which shall it be,
Doesn't much matter for duffers like me!

Two on the fairway, three-putt the green,
Six for my total, partner did same!
Next tee please be, kinder to me,
I'll do better, just wait and see!

I sadly progress, up to the nine,
Fifty the score, no rhythm, no rhyme!
Whack 'em and hack 'em, no change today,
Game gets worse, the harder I play!

Food cart lady watches our style,
Offers us hot dogs, suppresses a smile!
Did fine on the nine, but disaster on ten,
Haven't played this bad, since don't know when!

Found water next two, sand on thirteen,
Better go bowling, score's 'bout the same!
Whack 'em and hack 'em, try as I might,
Day soon over, club house in sight!

"Round the bend, lost ball on fifteen,
Bent my five iron, hitting a tree!
Sixteen and seventeen, more balls in the water,
Scared the ducks, sure made them scatter!

Eighteen par four, let's finish this right,
Best tee shot today, clear out of sight!
Two shots to green, game on the mend,
Long putt and short, par at the end!

Forget all the rest, ended up fine,
Celebrate tonight, fine wine and dine!
Whack 'em and hack 'em, next time we play,
All's well that ends well, glorious day!

Trips don't have to be clear across the country or the world to be fun; Denver is just one hour away! Sometimes Saturdays are meant to be enjoyed with no particular agenda; just go, have a good time, and enjoy each other's company. Anticipation is a wonderful thing!

Drivin' to Denver!

Drivin' to Denver, out on a spree, Saturday mornin', jus' you an' me!
Spiffy new car, delightful to heed, red with gold pinstripes, V-8 for speed!
Smooth on the highway, cruise control on, one hour to Denver, sunglasses don!
Radio's hummin'; we're singin' along, laughin' an' sharin', they're playin' our song!
Mountains in distance, snow against blue, grass in the valleys, sparklin' with dew!
Why go to Denver? Don't have a clue! Jus' Saturday mornin', spend time with you!

Ridin' to Denver, vast open spaces, no cares a-tall; we're off to the races!
So many choices, Denver has places, with nice friendly folks, smiles on their faces!
Sixteenth Street Mall, go if it pleases, we'll ride the trolley, feel the cool breezes!
Walkin' an' strollin', happy an' free, fun when we get there, jus' wait an' see!
Café by sidewalk, tables for show, we'll watch all the pigeons, struttin' so low!
Hot coffee in Denver, munch on a roll; bask in the sunshine, in mornin's gold glow!

Glidin' to Denver, see cows by the road, we're passin' up semis, trailers in tow,
Mesas touch sky, rocks gleaming gold, scrub oak on hillsides, nature's bold show,
Streams support beaver, dams and small ponds, eagles up high, jus' lookin' a-round,
Spyin' out country, like eagles we're fond, sights by the highway, with nature to bond!
Look up north; see the gold dome? By skyscrapin' buildings, business folks roam!
Almost to Denver, jus' let it be known, soon walkin' an' talkin', one hour from home!

Downtown in Denver, traffic will rush, we'll arrive at the mall; parkin's a fuss,
Car finally to rest, watch out for the bus! Listen to city, sounds meant for us,
We'll walk on the mall, look in each store; see trinkets an' fashions, in the glass door,
Shopkeepers know us, been here before, sometimes we buy, sometimes not sure,
Maybe come back, later this day; we'll count up our pennies, laughin' so gay,
Made it to Denver! Now time to play, mile high city, we'll spend Saturday!

Aloha! Hawaii waits for you and me! Honolulu Airport and the Wiki Wiki Bus, palm trees, the fresh scent of flowers, warm breezes, what a great start! Then it's off to baggage, rental cars, and Waikiki! Later, other islands beckon: Kauai, Maui, Lanai and the Big Island of Hawaii! Each has its own unique charm.

Hawaii is Waiting!

Look for an island, fly over seas,
Sunshine and orchids, warm tropical breeze!
Aloha will greet us and set us at ease,
Hawaii's is waiting for you and me!

Our jet will circle the island below,
Past white beaches and gentle surf flow!
Touch down on runway, taxi to gate,
Jetway to concourse, no need to wait!

Take Wiki Wiki to baggage and cars,
Sun sets in ocean, night brings the stars!
Ride to resort then settle in room,
Luau awaits us, drums beat a tune!

Beautiful people with shining black hair,
Drape us with lais, flowers scent the air!
Stroll to our table, fresh fruit and poi,
Roast pig and rice, dining's a joy!

Dancers with torches sway in the night,
Move from the shadows to golden firelight!
Hands tell a story of maidens so fair,
Love for the islands, o'hana who share!

Please take my hand, look deep in my eyes,
Hawaiian love song, under star-filled skies!
Walk slowly to room, the torches gold glow,
A night to remember, turn the lamp low!

Days in the sun, nights under moon,
Fine wine and dining, soft tropical tunes!
All this awaits, soon we will go,
By jet to the islands where trade winds blow!

Dream of the islands, in your mind's eye,
Sunshine and beaches and blue azure sky!
Aloha will greet us, just wait and see,
Hawaii's a-waitin', for you and me!

Rural Indiana and rural Hawaii have similarities. Folks in both states speak in easily recognizable dialects. In Indiana, it's a "Hoosier twang," in Hawaii, it's "Pidgin." Fishing, playful relations with the opposite sex, drinking beer, creating music, and other leisurely activities retain a level of importance not found in cities. Time passes at a much slower pace.

Like Hoosiers, storekeepers in rural Hawaii often have a very casual attitude toward business hours. Prospective customers can't change it, so relax, slow down, and come back later, on Hawaii time!

Hawaii Time!

Hawaii time, nanea ke la,
Island style, 'oihana a'ole le 'ale'a!
Wahine hiki alia, rather go play,
But haf' ta go work, maybe today!

Open da store, nine maybe ten,
Someday early, not sure when!
Few days open, 'bout twelve or so,
Rather go fishin', close up at fo'!

Closed all Sunday, but Saturday night,
Close at t'ree, Wahine delight!
Yesterday here, 'den someone call,
Lef' 'bout two, 'den not here a-tall!

Today been here, now haf' ta go,
Might come back, 'bout t'ree or so!
Close up early, jus' shut da do',
A'ole laka 'ia, dog guard da store!

Dog won't bite, a'ole da fear,
Nuttin' fo' steal, 'cept cooler da beer!
Ke maika'i dog, a-guardin' da place,
Dog trip da buggah, fall on da face!

Wahine a-waits, rather go play,
No want to work, leas' not today!
Island style, work no fun,
Hawaii time, enjoy da sun!

In 1992, Hurricane 'Iniki freed hundreds of domestic chickens from pens all over Kauai. Since then, they have proliferated in the wild to the point where they live all over the island. The darned things are everywhere! While they can be charming, they seem particularly stupid on Kauai. Roosters, hens and chicks act as if they own the roads, so watch out! Also, the roosters don't seem to know when they're supposed to crow, so they start at about 4:00 AM and continue all day long, just to make sure they have it covered! Inevitably, several of these colorful two-legged alarm clocks will live near where you are staying, and you will probably find yourself waking up *really* early!

Kauai Chicken

Kauai da place fo' chickens to be,
All da kine chickens from mountains to sea!
Chickens no worries, plenty to eat,
A-pickin' wild fruit, a-scratchin' da feet!

Big-ins and small-ins an' roosters dat crow,
A-strutin' an' cluckin' an' crossin' da road!
Hens wi' chicks, a-callin' peep-peep,
Outside my window, can't get to sleep!

No danger 'cept cars and maybe some hippie,
Free as da breeze, no wonder dey happy!
But chickens greet dawn, so we're awake too,
Thinkin' 'bout cookin', make chicken stew!

Hey chicken! Be pleased if quiet you stay,
Stop this a-crowin' a-greetin'da day!
A-little less noise by my sleepin' spot,
Or you' cream an' steam in my cookin' pot!

Breathtaking! Serene. Pristine! A lover's paradise! There are not enough appropriate descriptive phrases to characterize Hanalei Bay on the North shore of Kauai.

The beauty of Hanalei Bay has attracted an odd assortment of people. Many live in nearby Hanalei Town and Princeville. These include long-time locals (Kama'aina and locally born), itinerant surfers, new age types, celebrities and every other type of individual you can imagine. You're as likely to see locals driving a rusty pick-up truck held together with bungee cords and duct tape as to see a well-dressed older couple in a Mercedes or Cadillac. Take a stroll down the beach and you will understand!

Hanalei Bay

Hanalei Bay, gentle white wave,
Rhythm and pattern, soft music play!
Tropic gold beach, endless blue sea,
Green shadow mountains, beckon to me!

No hurry this day, Hawaii slow time,
Gently my mind, set words to rhyme!
Look through my eyes, what do you see?
Soul reaches out, it beckons to thee!

Read my thoughts as we stroll along,
Let voices entwine, now join in song!
Treasure each moment, lover's delight,
Hold my hand, walk 'til the night!

Stroll the beach; look to the sky,
Soul soars free, day drifts by!
Fluffy white clouds high in the blue,
Form faces, new places and poems for you!

Today in the sun, tonight under moon,
Breeze sings to lovers, surf hums the tune!
Surf swirls 'round, mixing the sand,
Cool sea breeze, warm touch your hand!

Perceive our future; peace we shall find,
Gold beach awaits, in fading sunshine!
Rest in memory, treasure this day,
Hanalei Bay, gentle white wave!

The road ends just past Hanalei Town. It is as if Kauai has said: "Stop, no further!" Soaring green cliffs begin, rising more than three thousand feet. Waterfalls pour over the cliffs and down into the sea. You have found the Na Pali.

The hardy among us can hike the Na Pali trail or paddle along the coast in a kayak. The more sedate (and risk-averse) can sign up for a powered catamaran ride that leaves from Hanalei Bay and sails along the Na Pali Coast. No matter how you do it, you will find that the Na Pali is a majestic, almost spiritual place. Linda and I did the hike (in the rain) and we sailed the catamaran. Recommend the catamaran!

Na Pali

Kauai adventure, island for fun,
Head for Na Pali, blue sky and sun!
Na Pali Coast wild, get ready for sea,
A glorious day to live and to be!

Leave Hanalei Bay, go with the flow,
Whitecaps on blue, morning sun glow!
Boat glides out, feel ocean spray,
Out past the reef, see dolphins at play!

Look down the coast, up three thousand feet,
Waterfall starts and plunges to sea!
Fish crest the waves, silver in foam,
Birds wing above, the sea their home!

Sail in a cave, ride the blue swell,
Dark and exciting, great story to tell!
In and around, then out to sea,
Treasure this moment, hold hands with me!

Anchor by cliffs, reef fish abound,
Snorkel and mask, see colors all 'round!
Red yellow blue, stripes white and black,
Dive to the bottom, quick look then back!

Storm clouds to port, get ready for sea,
Swells above mast, rocks to the lee!
Pack the gear, brave sea spray and gale,
Hang on tight, to harbor we sail!

Up on the wave, down in the trough,
Hard over helm, to lee white surf!
Na Pali wild ride, seek Hanalei Bay,
Safe through the channel, Oh what a day!

The Big Island of Hawaii is the current home of Pele', Goddess of Volcanoes. The current eruption emanates from the slopes and ridges on and near Kilauea. Linda and I observed lava flowing into the sea from the lowers slopes of Kilauea. At night, we watched the red glow deep in the main crater. Both scenes inspired awe and wonder at nature's raw power.

Yet there is another side to Kilauea, a green tropical side, a rain forest that rests uneasily near Pele's domain. We prefer the rain forest. There is cabin deep in the cool, misty and inviting forest, a place for lovers.

Kilauea Dream

Kilauea moe 'uhane, Hawaiian scene,
Misty and cool, rain forest green!
Hapu'u ferns greet tall koa trees,
Bright colored birds flit among leaves!

Clouds tower above, fluffy snow white,
Distant gray plume, Pele's delight!
Cabin in forest midst garden serene,
Call lovers to rest 'neath canopy green!

Hold my hand; stroll through the glade,
Eyes acquiesce, watch daylight fade!
Trade wind sighs a soft island tune,
Slack string guitar, voices that sooth!

Stars twinkle on, eyes twinkle too,
Reach out, touch, as lovers do!
Cabin waits in rain forest green,
Gladly to rest, my Kilauea dream!

The Kohala-Kona-Kailua Coast on the Big Island hosts some of the finest resorts in the world. The resorts rest along a narrow strip of land just back from the beaches; they present an oasis of tropical green along the edge of a volcanic desert that extends to the mountains on the inland side. The sun shines about 330 days each year; there is virtually no rain, and the green is maintained through constant irrigation. The Coast is a wonderful habitat for both tourists and Green Sea Turtles!

People love the beaches. So do the turtles. Hundreds of turtles feed on algae that grow on tidewater lava rocks; they also warm themselves on the sandy beaches right next to the tourists. Tourists, including me, enjoy watching the turtles. In turn, turtles watch the tourists, probably with some amusement!

Green Sea Turtles often live over one hundred years. They are travelers over the mighty Pacific Ocean, and they have learned to be quiet, gentle, peace-loving creatures. Have you ever looked long and deeply into the eyes of a Green Sea Turtle? Wisdom resides within!

Green Turtle

Turtle and me, on sand by the sea,
Five score years, he traveled the sea!
Miles and long life taught him to be,
Kindly, wise, and patient with me!

I looked in his eyes, this turtle so wise,
Our minds did meet and his song was sweet!
He explained many things, why love has wings,
Why happy hearts sing, and lovers share rings!

He said: "Peace from within, two become one,
Trust and belief, that's how it's done!
Love requires patience, be willing to bend,
Touch in the night and troubles will end!

Past is done, future is bright,
Hold hands, be glad, seek love's delight!
Two must share all that life brings,
Endless are rings when sharing begins!"

His song was sweet, my Green Turtle friend,
He slipped out to sea, but we'll meet again!
I'll travel the path he taught me to find,
Strive to be wise, patient and kind!

You do same, and love only me,
Together we'll seek a path from the sea!
Now leave the sand, walk hand in hand,
We cherish your thoughts, our Green Turtle friend!

All great vacations end. Drive back to the airport, get on a plane, and fly back to reality. However, we can always plan our next trip!

We're ready again! Leave cares and frustrations at home; pack summer clothes; and head for the airport. We're going south! Merry Christmas!

Two Old Fogies

Christmas for two, warm in the sun,
Two old fogies, out for some fun!
Fly away south, Disney World waits,
Cares disappear inside the gate!

Children all grown, no time for us,
So off on our own, avoid the fuss!
Mickey will greet us, just wait and see,
Laugh and be glad, lovers we'll be!

We'll stay at the Grand, expenses pre-paid,
Fine dining and roses, plans all made!
Castle and fireworks, view from our room,
White sand and palm trees, silver white moon!

Sleep late as we please, have breakfast for two,
Sip coffee, taste muffins, savor the fruit!
Concierge waits, we've been here before,
Updates our schedule; then opens the door!

Day in the sun, then dinner for two,
Candles and wine, hold hands with you!
Good Lord will smile, when evening comes,
For two old fogies, who had some fun!

6. SEASONS

Seasons come and seasons go, and our lives follow the annual rhythm. Work, play, conversations, indeed our very thoughts, move with the adjustments of the sun in the heavens. The seasons, spring, summer, fall and winter, present special moments and attractions to those who choose to perceive!

Let's start with spring! It is a time of renewal, blossoms, and emergence from a long winter indoors. Rejoice!

Spring Blossoms

When spring blossoms dot the grass an' treetops blush with green,
The songbirds start a-chirpin' to greet the morning scene!
The soft cool breeze at sunrise turns warm in golden glow,
And sparkling dew all silver helps the green lawn grow!
Geese an' ducks start headin' north to mate and nest and play,
We see their V-formations; they honk and quack all day!
It's time to think of plantin': potatoes, corn and beans,
When pansy colors spread all 'round an' treetops blush with green!

There's somethin' new and bold and fresh, in crispy springtime air,
And winter white has disappeared an' dawn breaks damp and fair!
See all the pussy willows, and feel the wholesome breeze,
And redwings in the cattails, a-callin' mates to please!
Some mornings start with rain showers, an' thunder roils on high,
But afternoons turn silver-blue, an' rainbows arc the sky!
We gladly purge our memories of winter's chilly scene,
When tulip petals open wide and treetops blush with green!

Late in cloud-sun morning, our neighbors venture out,
They marvel at the growin' flowers that peep all 'round about!
It sets my heart at ease when friends they come to call,
A-strollin' up the garden path, a-howdy to you all!
The morning sun warms your face, but coffee pipin' hot,
Would warm your hands and deep inside, man, it hits the spot!
Come on up; we'll sit outside; enjoy the springtime scene,
When daisies peek through the warming soil an' treetops blush with green!

We'll talk about spring plantin' and seeds we hope to grow,
And when the lawns need cuttin' and flowers that start to show!
Just plain an' simple talkin' like friends are bound to do,
I'll fill your coffee cup again and share my thoughts with you!
We'll say more with eyes and smiles and if such things can be,
We'll share rainbows in our minds for you and me to see!
It sends my soul a-soarin' in country morning dream,
When spring time flowers slow open and treetops blush with green!

Remember small towns, summer Sundays, Mom, Dad and a time before TV, video games and air conditioning? We tend to remember such times through a lens that has a rose-colored tint, but such times were special. Old folks like to walk down memory lane. Perhaps you younger folks will also enjoy our memories!

Small Town Summer Sunday

When Sunday mornin' touched the sky an' 'fore the sun burned hot,
Then all us kids would rise an' shine an' then jus' as like as not,
We'd all go lookin' for breakfast cookin'; it wuz sure to hit the spot!
Mom would serve up pancakes, with karo syrup on the side,
An' eggs fresh from Grandpa's farm an' bacon set beside!
Dad would share the funnies, with Lil' Abner an' Daisy Mae,
Dagwood, Blondie an' Snuffy Smif, we'd laugh to start our day!
After Sunday breakfast, we'd help clean up the mess,
An' wash syrup off our faces, an' dress in Sunday best!

Church wuz walkin' distance, an' 'fore the sun burned hot,
We'd all walk down to service, an' then jus' as like as not,
Preacher'd smile an' greet us, then preach to hit the spot!
He'd drone on 'bout sin an' such, an' we'd fidget in our seats,
Mom would say "amen" a-lot, an' Dad would fall asleep!
Sunday school for all us kids wuz held in the church alcove,
Behind a big drawn curtain, we'd giggle an' eyes would rove!
Teacher would try her level best an' tell 'bout love an' all,
Suppose it made sense to some, but we'd think 'bout playin' ball!

When Sunday church wuz over an' the noonday sun burned hot,
We'd all head on home a-walkin' an' then jus' as like as not,
Mom would fix Sunday dinner; it wuz sure to hit the spot!
She'd wash an' peel some taters, an' boil up fresh sweet corn,
An' slice up ripe tomaters, garden picked that very morn!
Then Mom would fix a-chicken, an' roast it golden brown,
Dad would baste that chicken an' lay some biscuits down!
Then Dad would set the table an' lay out our Sunday spread,
Mom would call to one an' all: "It's time you-all got fed!"

When Sunday dinner ended an' evenin' sun burned hot,
Dad would walk us down to town an' then jus' as like as not,
He'd buy us each an ice cream cone, an' boy that hit the spot!
Our trick wuz to lick an' lick, but drips would fall right down,
We'd freeze lips on double dips then all walk back through town!
It wuz our special family treat, when Sunday sun went low,
We'd head back home with ice cream, an' boy that stole the show!
We'd skip along with sticky smiles and laugh an' run an' play,
Dad and Mom would talk and frown an' plan for work next day!

When we got home we'd take baths in washtub water hot,
Behind the stove in kitchen cove, and jus' as like as not,
Mom would scrub an' rinse us down, an' she didn't miss a spot!
We'd all dress in summer wear, and comb the tangles out,
All spic and span an' then we ran to Dad an' all about!
He'd laugh an' say: "I declare, I've never seen such kids,
Who laugh an' play the day away, what will you-all do next?"
After awhile we'd settle down an' watch summer sun fade low,
Then lightnin' bugs would dance aroun' and make the evenin' glow!

Sunday night wuz special, though late evenin' air stayed hot,
We'd gather 'round the radio, an' then jus' as like as not,
Jack Benny would start at seven an' boy he hit the spot!
Amos an' Andy were all up next, Kingfish would be absurd,
Bergen an' McCarthy followed, along with Mortimer Snerd!
Long 'bout eight we'd all be tired, but not yet ready for sleep,
But Mom would tuck us in an' ask: "Lord their souls please keep!"
A perfect night for summer Sunday; the stars would all come out,
Our door would close; we would doze; the Lord had blessed our house!

Fall colors accent a time of fulfillment; flowers have gone to seed, farmers bring in their crops, and creatures of the woods and fields wear winter coats. The mountains gleam with golden aspen trees against a blue and white cloud sky!

When Aspen Trees Turn Golden

When aspen trees turn golden and frost replaces dew,
And birds begin a-gatherin' in skies mixed gray an' blue,
A cool fall breeze a-blowin' and treetops softly moan,
Crickets chirp less often, and bees have all gone home!
The geese fly V-formation; they sail across the sky,
See 'um from our window as they honk and pass us by!
It's time to sip hot coffee and snuggle close to you,
When aspen trees turn golden and frost replaces dew!

There's something wholesome special about the atmosphere,
When summer flowers have faded and colored leaves are here!
We miss of course the blossoms and green upon the trees,
And buzzin' of the insects and summer's warming breeze!
But the air's so crisp and clean, the snow's on mountains high,
They rise to greet the morning with clouds in deep blue sky!
It's a picture sent from heaven, fresh and special new,
When aspen leaves turn golden and frost replaces dew!

The breeze takes leaves a-swirlin' across the faded grass,
And people dress in jackets, a-wavin' as they pass!
It sets my heart a-smiling; friends have come to call,
A-strollin' up the sidewalk a-howdy to you all!
I know the breeze is nippin' at hair upon your heads,
Your hands down deep in pockets, your ears are pinky-red!
Come on in we'll sit a spell; coffee's on to brew,
When aspen trees turn golden and frost replaces dew!

We'll talk about the weather, when snow will come this year,
How the kids are doin' and plans for Christmas cheer!
Just passin' on such simple thoughts 'tween sips of coffee hot,
Have just one more cup my friend; it's bound to hit the spot!
I don't know how to tell it, but if such a thing could be,
I'd invite my friends the angels to sit and talk with me!
It sets my heart a-ticking, shared thoughts 'tween me and you,
When aspen trees turn golden and frost replaces dew!

Crystals swirl in a cloudy sky; the frosty air nips at your nose, and the snow crunches under foot. Winter!

When Snow Flies Silent

When snow flies silent through the air, white crystals all around,
Gray-black trees stand here and there, above the pure white ground!
The winter chill creeps to my bones, and your nose is rosy-red,
Sparkles fall from winter sky, land gently on your head!
A gentle breeze stirs up the snow and hisses 'cross the grass,
Swirling figures dance in gray, pale ghostly, quick to pass!
It's time to watch in quiet awe and nature makes no sound,
When snow flies silent through the air, white crystals all around!

There's somethin' kind of special about this time of year,
When we enjoy the quiet and plan for Christmas cheer!
Of course we miss fall colors and swirling wind-blown leaves,
And honkin' of the south-bound geese a-wingin' on the breeze!
But now we have a winter scene, white both high and low,
Come with me; we'll walk awhile, amongst the crystal snow!
Our footsteps leave a trail behind and make a crunching sound,
When snow flies silent in the air, white crystals all around!

The winter snow damps all the noise of man's activities,
And people move more slowly amongst the gray-black trees!
They all dress in hats and coats; they greet us as we pass,
And breezes swirl the pure white snow a-cross the silver path!
When we're cold we'll go inside and sit beside the fire,
And snuggle close and then confide what hearts now true desire!
The glowing coals will warm our bones; we'll hear the crackling sound,
When snow flies silent through the air, white crystals all around!

We'll talk about the future, when spring will come next year,
And sip warm apple cider, it will sparkle gold and clear!
We'll dream great dreams of glory, beside the fire at ease,
And snow outside will waft our thoughts to heaven on the breeze!
I don't know how to say it, but just 'tween you and me,
I love what's out the window, a wonderland to see!
It warms my heart just thinkin'; my thoughts spin all around,
When snow flies silent through the air, white crystals on the ground!

Christmas season seems to start earlier each year, with garish lights, store shelves piled high with "stuff," and people rushing all about. It all seems so frantic, so shallow, and so devoid of the true spirit of Christmas! Perhaps we all should take a moment to reflect and look in memory's window!

Christmas Season

When Christmas season hits its stride with all its glitzy sights,
Carols ring out so insincere; stores glow in garish lights!
Small kids ride in shopping carts; Moms try oh so hard,
To satisfy their every whim, with maxed out credit cards!
Tempers flare, shrill horns blare; cars and stoplights meet,
A frantic pace, the cars do race, through slush on icy streets!
We make such a fuss; it's all of us; we shop 'til late at night,
When Christmas season hits its stride with all its glitzy sights!

When I got home last evening, away from noise and fights,
I made hot tea and tried to see beyond bright city lights!
Memories gleamed from long ago, a simpler time and place,
I saw a house and countryside; life flowed at a slower pace!
The scene evolved to Christmas Eve, ice crystals all around,
Moonlit woods, pure white snow, and not a single sound!
I looked deep in memory's sleep and saw a golden light;
The light glowed 'round a woman, in soft and gentle night!

Then I became a boy again, next to this woman wise,
There was no fuss, just two of us, behold her twinkling eyes!
I touched her hand; it was warm; she smiled and said to me,
"Meaning lies beyond the skies; look up and try to see!"
"Open your memory window; see above the pure white snow,
What does Christmas really mean, beyond the city glow?"
I looked up beyond the heavens; a star glowed in the east,
I saw a deeper meaning; God's gift for Christmas Eve!

So when Christmas season hits, turn your lights down low,
Find a deeper meaning, above the pure white snow!
Our Lord was born so long ago; God's true gift was given,
In the east a star will glow, it's just beyond the heaven!
A wise old woman told me, and I believe it's true,
We give gifts to remember, God's gift to me and you!
So let's not fuss, let's all of us, look out in deepest night,
When Christmas season comes again, a star will bring delight!

An idyllic view of daily farm life can only be dreamed by city folk; the reality is quite different. Yet on certain days and times of year, the reality has a special quality. The singing birds at sunrise, the myriad colors of leaves in the fall, the ordered fields and fencerows, the sound of whippoorwills at night and the stark beauty of winter snow on the landscape are indeed special to those who choose farm life. Between chores, there are also opportunities to hunt small game, run trap lines and explore the ever-changing countryside. Join me and enjoy verses that describe spring, summer, fall and winter in the country!

Country Seasons

The country side's a-waitin,' for you and me to go,
Tramping or'e hill and station, no cares this world to know.
Pale green leaves of springtime, fields of planted corn,
Pastures gleam in sunshine, the dew of early morn!

A good time to be livin', in tune with nature's way,
Spring shower or'e hill a-comin', to grow the corn and hay.
Oh! I like springtime best, except for winter, summer, fall,
God's own time of promise to creatures great and small!

The summer sun's a-waitin', for you and me to go,
Tramping or'e hill and station, the summer breeze to know.
Fencerows full of blossoms, fields of tasseled corn,
Pastures deep in grasses, birds singing greet the morn!

A good time to be livin' in tune with nature's way,
Summer breeze so gentle, ripples grass in endless wave.
Oh! I like summer best, except for winter spring and fall,
Glory in its fullness, creatures great and small!

The autumn's gold's a-waitin', for you and me to go,
Tramping or'e hill and station, frost on hill does glow.
Gold-red leaves in sunshine, fields of ripened grain,
Harvest time's a-comin', fill barns and cribs to brim!

A good time to be livin', in tune with nature's way,
Season to fruition, gather while we may.
Oh! I like autumn best, except for winter spring and all,
Harvest will be bringing, food for winter's call!

The winter's cold a-waitin', for you and me to go,
Tramping or'e hill and station, crunching through the snow.
Silence of the winter, fields of dazzling white,
Crystals dancing in the air, greet the morning light!

Moonlight through the window, pale shadows everywhere,
I'd never think of leavin' my family's loving care.
Oh! I like winter best, except for summer, spring and fall,
God's own time for us to rest by fireside warmth and glow!

Country ways are busy, for you and me to grow,
To love each special season, nature's ways to show.
Join me now in praising, country season's all,
Different than the city, for creatures great and small!

Autumn is special to me because it matches my current season of life. September is here, and I choose to enjoy the fruits of long labor, high on the mountain, with the person I love!

High on the Mountain

High on the mountain, golden leaves glow, frost on tall grasses, a forecast for snow.
Ravens and blue jays call to their mates, songbirds are silent, migration awaits!

Pale sun, swift clouds, cool breezes blow, stirring the aspens, they moan soft and low.
Time of fulfillment, wild flowers to seed, long summer's over, before winter's need!

We've sowed and reaped; cares are laid by, others must strive; we smile and sigh.
We've scaled our mountain, now survey the scene; leaves flutter and fall; what does it mean?

Look to the heavens, past clouds and sun, tired we be, but the race was won.
Heaven will wait, peace we now seek, walk hand in hand, on top of the peak!

My eyes twinkle; you give me a smile, we'll sit by the path and rest for awhile.
Night will come and soft darkness lie, then fly to the stars, high in the sky!

What happens when seasons end? One day each of us will find out; but for now we can only imagine!

Seasons' Song

The seasons past each one I know, in memory soft I watch them flow; September's here; soon time will show the winter cold and drifting snow!

Seasons come and seasons go; a time for blossoms, a time to know, a time for love, a time for play, a time to work from day to day!

That all has passed and soon we'll see, through crystal glass a golden scene; heaven waits above the strife, Elysian Fields and eternal life!

Seasons come and season go; I love you still and we both know; soon we'll feel the cold winds blow; we'll stop and watch the drifting snow!

While we wait be patient dear; just hold my hand and do not fear; hand in hand we'll drift along and play our roles to season's song!

7. GROWIN' UP COUNTRY!

Growin' up country in the 1940s and 50s produced kids with a unique set of attitudes, values and habits. We were trained by parents, schools and community to be self-reliant, hard-working and for the most part, easy-going. Farm boys of my generation typically drove tractors before they were twelve. We quickly learned dozens of uses for baling wire. Country girls like my sisters often started supper as soon as they got home from school and before Mom got home from her town job. Washin' and ironin' on Saturdays and pickin' beans and other garden vegetables in the summer were routine chores.

Even now, after moving to the city, we tend to be self-starters. We lead busy lives. We often smile in an "aw shucks" kind of way, and we are shy around strangers. We like country music, blue jeans with straight legs, and pick-up trucks. In so many ways, we retain our country roots. You can take the kid out of the country....

After over 50 years of city life, I often think and dream about my early years on the farm. In this chapter, my poems reminisce about growin' up country. Perhaps they will strike sympathetic chords in the memories of you former farm kids. For you folks who were raised in the city, the poems might provide insight into a very special way of life. In either case, enjoy!

Country Memories!

When mornin' blushes pale an' blue upon the hill so green,
I think about my country youth an' face the new day scene!
My countryside's a-waitin', turns warm in golden glow,
See the crystal dew all over; it helps the memories grow!
The farm boys I remember; they started their chores at dawn,
Hear cowbells softly clankin'; see calves on barnyard lawn!
It was a place for growin' up, to know the hills so green,
See mornin' come with golden sun upon my country scene!

There's somethin' bold an' bright an' fresh in country air,
And city noise fades away when dawn breaks damp and fair!
See straight an' ordered fencerows; feel the cool dawn breeze,
An' meadow lark upon green branch a-callin' mate to please!
Some mornin's start with rain showers; thunder roils on high,
But in my mind it's silver-blue, an' white clouds dot the sky!
I gladly purge my troubled thoughts; toils an' what they mean,
When country sun peeps over hill to greet the new day scene!

When evenin' comes I think in sums 'bout the crops that grow,
An' when the hay needs cuttin', an' corn shoots start to show!
Jus' plain an' simple thinkin', like the farmers always do,
Guess I'll go to supper; an' share Mom's pie with you!
We'll reminisce 'bout rainbows, in mind for both to see,
An' we'll finish pie with coffee, for if such things can be!
When evenin' comes with settin' sun, soft breezes move the air,
Come on up, you're welcome, in memories bright an' fair!

When evenin' fades upon the glade, stars an' moon come out,
I'll marvel at the Milky Way an' heaven all round about!
It sets a troubled heart at ease when night dreams come to call,
An' angels fly all 'round about, an' shootin' stars they fall!
Contentment now and promise, a new day we'll surely win,
Crops will grow an' we will know the grand an' glorious plan!
So join me in gold memories, in my countryside so green,
When night ends and mornin' brings a bright an' glorious scene!

Remember the hayloft? When the neighbor boys and I were pre-teens, the hayloft provided adventure and just plain fun! We would climb up the ladder to the loft above the cow stalls on rainy afternoons when outdoor chores were put aside, and we would jump and slide, play hide and seek, Cowboys and Indians, sample Five Brothers Chewing Tobacco (only once, it made us sick), and roll around in the hay until supper time.

Of course, we would get all itchy and eventually have to wash off at the pump by the house before we were allowed in for supper, but we had great times. Remember?

The Hayloft

The old barn loft was the place to play for three farm boys on a rainy day!
Hay's so soft, it smelled so sweet; we jumped and played, no shoes on feet!
The cows below looked up amazed, at three farm kids who jumped in hay.
We didn't care; it was fun you see, to toss the hay and laugh with glee!

The kids in town paid for fun; ours was free; we'd jump and run!
We would rather share in loft up there, than in town or anywhere.
Grandma came; she looked and smiled, kids in loft, free and wild.
Her eyes twinkled, for in her youth, she played in loft, like us in truth.

I remember the days gone by, when life was simple, no twists, no lies.
It was great fun, wild and free, to toss sweet hay and laugh with glee!
If world could learn from farm kid's ways, joy of life, in simple play.
A better place for all would be, to jump in hay and put cares away!"

My two sisters and I have all gone our separate ways since high school in Hymera Indiana. Oh, we keep in touch by phone and we send Christmas cards. Since our parents passed on, family visits are rare. Still, we occasionally reminisce on the phone about the old days.

I think about my sisters often. Memories especially come to the fore on rainy spring afternoons when I relax in an easy chair by the fireplace. The rain patters gently, the fire glows, and I close my eyes.

Sisters

The rain is gently falling; it's a dreamy kind of day,
I hear robins gently calling, my work is laid away.
I think of my two sisters, as the evening turns to night,
My memories soft and tender, as tranquil they delight.
Memories we three share, though we have taken different ways,
May the good Lord bless and keep you, 'til the ending of our days!

Remember Christmas in the country? In the time before television, farm families typically spent Christmas Eve at home. Older folks sometimes shared stories about the "old days." Kids listened, there were few distractions.

I remember one story about a very special Christmas Eve. It was told by a Great Grandfather, who was nearly 90 years old when I was a boy. The following poem tells a version of the story as I remember it. The setting is an Indiana farm before the turn of the twentieth century.

Christmas Eve

"The eve before Christmas, snow on the ground,
Dark woods, white fields, nary a sound.
Up from the barn, chores are all done,
Long shadows creep from pale winter sun.

Lights in the house, but barnyard was dark,
My Father helped Mother, dinner to start.
Took the milk to the porch, filtered it out,
It would set overnight, cream to the top.

Out of barn boots, cleaned up the mess,
Combed tangled hair, washed hands and face.
Walked in the kitchen, it was full of gold light,
My Mother at stove, a new recipe tonight!

Stockings were hung on the mantle with care,
By Mother and Father, with presents to share.
Add one for Grandma; she's still on our minds,
Her passing hit hardest, at holiday time.

A small sugar pine, away from the stove,
Served as our tree, it was Christmas you know.
Popcorn on thread, rapped round and round,
Hand-made ornaments from things we found.

Mom and my sisters, the table they set,
I set napkins; they were linen, our best!
Candles on table, oil lamps on the mantle,
Love passed 'round, all we could handle!

Then we set out a feast, food from our farm,
Roast duck and gravy, green beans and corn,
Poured cool tart cider, fresh from the shed,
Blackberry pie, whipped cream all spread.

No King could ask more, we sat down to eat,
Father gave blessing, all thankful were we.
Then Father told jokes; we all laughed aloud,
Mother's eyes twinkled; wrinkles smoothed out.

After our dinner, the mess was cleaned up,
Except for the pie, we could not get enough!
Father asked quiet, Mother opened a sack,
She brought out treasures, held nothing back.

Sets of new socks for Father and me,
New cotton dresses, for sisters to see.
An apple and pear for each of us kids,
Mother's sweet smile meant more than gifts.

It was time for gifts for Mother to see,
A new store-bought shawl from Father and me,
My sisters were handy, used needle and thread,
Made warm mittens, hand-knitted, they said.

Mother thanked us, her love we all shared,
She said: "the best gift was all being here!
Remember first Christmas," she said with a smile,
"Our good Lord was born; it's been quite awhile,

Go to the window, and silent please be,
Dim all the lights, and look to the east.
See the far hill, all covered with snow?
Look over trees, what does night show?"

We did as she said, eyes adjusted to night,
And over the trees, a spectacular sight!
It was the brightest star we ever did see!
It gleamed in the sky, a wondrous scene!

Glory to God, on that Christmas Eve,
Farm family together, in silent dream.
Later I climbed upstairs to my to nest,
The hour was late, and I needed my rest.

Snug in my bed, I pondered a bit,
Mother was special, wisdom her gift.
I will never forget that wondrous night,
When Mother showed heaven's own light!"

When I was a boy, I would walk the woods and pastures by myself. Late summer afternoons and evenings after chores were special. Typically, I would wear patched blue jeans, but no shirt. Of course, shoes were unnecessary.

Away from the barn and open water, bugs that bite usually weren't a problem. Grasshoppers, June bugs, cicadas, and dozens of other chirping and buzzing insects somehow added background music to nature's timeless scene. I didn't mind the bugs.

Gentle summer breezes would stir the tall trees and ripple the grass on the hilltops in endless waves. Sometimes I would find a special hilltop, sit on a convenient boulder away from the chiggers in the grass, and view my country kingdom! When evening came, I would rise up, walk past a small lake, and head toward the lighted house that was home!

When I was Young!

"The world was new when I was small,
The sun gleamed bright, the trees stood tall!
I knew no words for stream and stone,
I named them all and walked alone!

I gave names to hills and dells
And looked deep in wishing wells.
I sat at night by silver mere,
And saw the moon and stars appear!

Points of light, stars circled round,
Above my head, they formed a crown.
A king I was in small domain,
Small creatures bowed and knew my name!

The world was fair when I was small,
Full of promise and love for all.
Home light bright when evening came,
Off to bed and pleasant dream!

Mom was there, with soothing song,
Dreams we shared, our hearts were one.
She held my hand and read my soul,
All my hopes, she smiled, she knows!

A king I was on pillow throne,
Warm in bed, my spirit roamed.
Mon did guide, she showed the way,
To magic lands, 'til light of day!"

Growin' up country wasn't all "peaches and cream!" Every day, morning and night, farm animals had to be tended. Cows, hogs, chickens, goats, even a few horses, had to be fed and otherwise cared for.

Cows were a special pain; they had to be milked. In the forties and fifties, most milking on small farms was still done by hand. Hands and forearms were thoroughly tired by the time the milker got to the third or fourth cow. On our farm, we had between three and six! Guess who did the milkin'?

Cows do four things: they eat, produce calves and milk, and they also produce manure. For some reason known only to cows, manure, tons of it each year, mostly gets produced inside the barn! Guess who cleaned the barn?

Even today, after 50 years, I'm not sure which life lesson was taught by milkin' cows and cleanin' barns! In any case, consider the following poem about this "special" set of farm chores.

Milkin' Time!

Trek to barn to start each morn as gold light touches trees,
Country chores, out of doors, smell that mornin' breeze!
The cows a-doin' always mooin', just open up their gate,
To their stalls along the walls, their milkin' jus' can't wait!

Put feed an' hay in manger, then lock the stanchions down,
Wash bottom to top, slip an' slop, hooves a-stampin' 'round!
So line the pails up by the rails; then start with one old cow,
Tired hands a-workin' tail a-swishin', get rhythm goin' now!

Set full pail by the rail, then move on to cow marked two,
Old two jus' shifts, what a witch! Her milk is thin an' blue!
Don't know why she's kept alive, bet she'd make good stew,
But in any case, have to race; got three more cows to do!

Then pour the milk through filters, keep it nice an' clean,
Take tall can to coolin' stand, it will separate the cream!
Raise stanchion noose, turn cows loose, out the gate they rove,
Now my turn 'fore breakfast burns, it's sittin' by the stove!

After wash and coffee slosh, change to clean school clothes,
School bus comin' gotta be runnin' my how time it flows!
Five miles away, road not paved, bus bouncin' we all go,
In town arrive, still alive, 'bout eight fifteen or so!

Town kids arrive; they're not shy; dressed so neat they smile,
We jus' watch, in jeans an' such, dressed in country style!
We shuffle shoes to shake off blues, an' rub off country mud,
Barnyard smell, oh what the hell, despite the soap and suds!

Then classes start, words impart, teachers drone on an' on,
Girls they flirt; boys get hurt; they stare and blush an' fawn,
Yet some do learn, ambitions burn, not all was hormone play,
Dreams were born, not all forlorn, school it meant escape!

At school day end we would wend, from town to country station,
No time to roam, must get home, the cows were always waitin'!
Start the chores, clean barn floors, before the cows come in,
Wash them down, another round, it's milkin' time again!

Remember the 4-H pledge? "I pledge my head to clearer thinking, my heart to greater loyalty, my hands to greater service, and my health to better living…" and so on. On farms and in small towns across America, 4-H clubs still thrive. Kids raise calves, pigs, and horses. They grow vegetables and build electric motors. They sew dresses and bake cakes. The 4-H Clubs of America provide opportunities for rural kids to complete satisfying projects, socialize, enter their products in county and state fairs, and go to summer camps for a (very) few days in the summer.

I belonged to a local club in Lyford Indiana for two years, before we moved to a larger, more remote farm. Four-H was and still is a wonderful organization!

Four-H Rhyme

Country rhyme in four-H time, makes the work seem fun,
Raise the calf, more work by half, but do what must be done!

The girls take part, kitchen art, work for home skills sake,
Can berries blue, pumpkins too, an' bake that special cake!

Country skills not city frills, yet social life means fun,
To county fair, learn an' share, prizes can be won!

For country kids, hear the bids, for calf that's now mature,
Satisfaction, auction action, but hate to part with her!

Learn the lesson, 'bout life's short session, from birth to life to death,
Be glad for time with country rhyme and head, heart, hands and health!

When I was a boy, Parke County Indiana was "the popcorn capital of the world," or so local farmers said. I suppose it's still true.

In any case, when I was 10 and 11, popcorn fields extended up to our home in Lyford, Parke County, Indiana. In the fall, I would go into the fields after the farmers harvested with mechanical pickers and look for the remnant ears of popcorn. Turn rows at the ends of fields were particularly lucrative spots. A full morning in a field usually resulted in a bushel or so of perfectly good popcorn!

The leftover popcorn was put to good use. My sisters and I would shell and clean it and measure it out, one pound per measure. We then put each measure of popcorn in a "penny" brown paper bag.

On Saturdays, Mom would drop me off in Clinton with a gunny sack full of one-pound bags. I would walk from house to house and sell popcorn for twenty-five cents per bag. On some Saturdays, my sisters and I would make five or six dollars! My thoughts at the time ran as follows.

Pickin' Up Popcorn

Go out back, old gunny sack, in popcorn time of the season,
Start cold morn 'fore sun gets warm, makin' money's the reason!

With sun rise flow fields do glow, ground will warm an' thaw,
Get done fast, cold won't last, walkin' gets muddy an' slow!

Back to home, full field combed, bushel of corn for the workin',
Shell an' clean it, measure an' bag it, my fingers are all a-hurtin'!

Sell in town for a quarter per pound, a-walkin' door to door,
Folks will buy if I really try, an' cash makes spirit soar!

Profits do grow 'cause cost is low, no need to pay for labor,
For kids like me, labor is free, profits all ours to savor!

Share with sisters, all got blisters, five or six dollars all told,
Save mine in a jar, hope to buy car, when I'm sixteen an' old!

As I grow older, I think a lot about my early days. I know that most folks, including me, prefer to dwell on pleasant memories. Perhaps heaven really is just a home in the country!

Goin' Home!

Getting' old, not so bold, our path a golden haze,
Walk with you, lovers true, we'll share our ending days!

Stay on path, death will pass, then free as the summer breeze,
Look on down without a frown, a-smilin' through the trees!

When time comes, we won't run, we've reaped our earthly bounty,
In Elysian field, souls will yield; heaven's a home in the country!

EPILOGUE

All things end. So it now ends with this little book of poems. However, more poems reside in my mind and heart; these will be brought forth as time permits. For now, I hope the foregoing poems brought lots of smiles and perhaps an occasional tear! Best wishes, and may the Good Lord keep you until we meet again!

ABOUT THE AUTHOR

Frank and Linda Gertcher were born and raised in small towns and on farms in the Midwest: Linda in Iowa and Frank in Indiana. Although they call the lovely city of Colorado Springs home, they have not forgotten their roots; they are both Midwestern farm kids deep down inside! "You can take the kid out of the country…"

Linda provides much of the inspiration for Frank's writing. According to Frank: "Linda excites and amuses me, and she warms my old heart! We walk our golden path; we laugh and love; we anticipate, and we plan. She brings meaning to my life! We are fortunate; in our autumn years, we can travel. Life is good!"

In addition to "Wind Grass Hill and Other Poems," Frank wrote "Shaman on Wind Grass Hill." Published in 2009 by Black Rose Writing, this novel tells the inspirational and romantic stories and describes the spiritual journeys of several generations of

Shamans. These special people continue to live in rural southern Indiana. They are as much a part of the land as the Wabash River, the woodlands and the farms of the Midwest.

Upcoming titles are as follows:

Fox Tales from Wind Grass Hill
Dark Cabin under Wind Grass Hill
Small Voices from Wind Grass Hill

LaVergne, TN USA
07 May 2010
181799LV00004BD/1/P

9 781935 605287